The ■Carol Retirement Handbook

SECOND EDITION

AGE Concern **BOOKS**

© 1997 Age Concern England
Published by Age Concern England
1268 London Road
London SW16 4ER

First published 1993
Second edition published 1997

Design and production Eugenie Dodd
Printed in Great Britain by Bell & Bain Ltd, Glasgow

A catalogue record for this book is available
from the British Library.

ISBN 0–86242–237–X

While every effort has been made to check the accuracy
of material contained in this publication, Age Concern
England cannot accept responsibility for the results of any
action taken by readers as a result of reading this book.

Age Concern England is pleased to offer customised
editions of all its titles to UK companies, institutions
or other organisations wishing to make a bulk purchase.
For further information, please contact the Publishing
Department at the address on this page. Tel: 0181-679 8000.
Fax: 0181-679 6069. E-mail: addisom@ace.org.uk

Contents

Staying healthy 133

Special needs 169

Bereavement 188

Further information 197

Introduction

Some people eagerly look forward to retirement, some dread it; most people probably fall somewhere between these two extremes. Whatever your attitude, however positive your feelings, retirement is a time of adjustment – and adjustment is not always easy.

Retirement may mean that you have more control over your life than ever before: the 50 or so hours that were taken up by work and travelling to work are now yours to spend as you like. But being able to do exactly as you like with your time can seem almost a burden. The fact that you are working can sometimes provide convenient excuses:

► I have always wanted to take up painting but I never have time.

► I know I'm very unfit but I'm always too busy and tired to do anything about it.

► I know the house needs a lot doing to it, but I seem to spend the whole weekend just catching up.

Leaving work strips away all these excuses at once. Whereas an extra couple of hours a day free might have seemed like an unqualified bonus, having the whole week free to spend as you choose may seem positively daunting.

Retirement often causes stresses in people's relationships. One partner may retire and want to embark on all sorts of joint activities while the other is still working and too busy to take on anything extra. Couples who have been married 30 or 40 years may find their relationship under strain if they are suddenly thrown together for 24 hours a day. You may find yourselves having to work out afresh how you are going to live together, just as you did when you were first married.

People who live alone may worry about missing the day-to-day companionship provided by going to work. People who are disabled or in poor health may feel anxious about how they will cope as they get older and frustrated by being unable to do all the things they had hoped to do.

Many employers provide retirement courses for their employees. In addition to providing practical information and suggestions, these can give people a chance to talk about their hopes and expectations, their fears and anxieties. Some courses include people's partners.

This book aims to provide people who are about to retire or have just retired with suggestions and practical information that will be useful for the years ahead.

Chapter 1 looks at the various aspects of managing your money, as having an adequate income is essential whatever your plans for the future. Chapter 2 looks at ways of using your time, including educational opportunities, doing voluntary work, earning money, and travel. Chapter 3 discusses the issue of whether or not to move house – perhaps even abroad. It also covers repairs and maintenance.

Staying as healthy as possible is vital if you are to get the most out of retirement. Chapter 4 looks at positive steps you can take to maintain – or even improve – your health. It also looks at sexuality, and certain health problems which may affect older people.

Anyone can find themselves in the position of having to arrange for one of their parents to receive support services at home – or even go into a care home – and all of us will at some stage have to cope with bereavement, and the various practical tasks that have to be undertaken after a death. These are the subjects of Chapters 5 and 6.

Because of the limitations of space the information given cannot be detailed or comprehensive. The aim is to outline the main points for each topic and then to point readers in the right direction to obtain more information if they need it.

But the aim of this book is not simply to provide information. It aims also to encourage – to encourage you to make the most of the opportunities offered by retirement, to regard retirement in a positive light, to see it not as the closing of one door but as the opening of many.

Managing money

'How well off am I going to be?' is a question that is likely to concern anyone on the verge of retirement. Whatever your plans, they are likely to depend to some extent on the state of your finances.

- Pensions and benefits
- Your tax position
- Your savings and investments
- Boosting your income
- Shopping
- Making a Will
- Managing another person's money

When considering your financial position, there are certain questions it is worth asking yourself: Are you receiving all the pensions and benefits you are entitled to? Are you paying more tax than you should? Could your savings be better invested? Is there anything you can do to boost your income?

This chapter looks at all these issues. It also looks at shopping, and how to ensure that you get value for your money when you come to spend it, and at making a Will and managing another person's money.

£

Pensions and benefits

If you have an occupational pension, this may well be a significant source of income once you leave work. In addition, most people receive a State Retirement Pension. People who are self-employed, and employees who did not belong to a company scheme, may have a personal pension. This section looks at these three types of pension, and at the various State benefits that are available to people with low incomes and to people with disabilities and their carers.

Occupational pensions

There are two main types of occupational pension scheme:

SALARY-RELATED SCHEMES give a pension based on a proportion of final earnings – typically either $\frac{1}{60}$ or $\frac{1}{80}$ of your final salary for each year worked. Two-thirds of final salary is generally the maximum pension possible. Often only part of your pay is pensionable – check in your scheme booklet. How well your pension keeps up with inflation will depend on whether or not it is index-linked.

MONEY-PURCHASE SCHEMES give a pension based on the value of the pension fund you have built up. The contributions you and your employer pay are invested, and the proceeds of the fund are used to buy an annuity (a lifetime pension). The amount of the annuity will depend on how well the investments have done, how long you have been paying into the pension fund, and annuity rates at the time you draw your pension.

Contracted in or out?

Occupational pension schemes can be 'contracted in' or 'contracted out' of the State Earnings-Related Pension Scheme (SERPS – described on p 16). Members of contracted-in schemes will receive their occupational pension on top of SERPS. Members of contracted-out schemes will pay lower National Insurance contributions and receive an occupational pension instead of the State Additional Pension.

Until April 1997, members of a contracted-out salary-related scheme had to receive a minimum amount called the Guaranteed Minimum Pension (GMP): this is broadly equivalent to the State Additional Pension you would have received if you had stayed in SERPS. However, for any pension that builds up after April 1997, the scheme does not have to provide a specific GMP; instead schemes have to meet certain conditions in order to be contracted out of SERPS.

FACTFILE

▶ There are over 10.6 million people of pensionable age in the UK (60 or over for women, 65 or over for men).

▶ This comprises roughly 18 per cent of the population.

▶ In 1995 there were 6,911,000 women and 3,740,000 men of pensionable age.

If you belong to a money-purchase scheme you will have Protected Rights, which may be more or less than the Additional Pension you would have received.

The lump sum

With both types of scheme you have the option of taking a certain amount as a lump sum and getting a lower pension. Your pension will be treated as taxable earnings but the lump sum is tax-free, so it is usually advisable to take the maximum lump sum. However, if you belong to a good index-linked scheme, it may be better to take a higher pension rather than the lump sum.

Collecting former employers' pensions

If you have changed jobs in the past, you may have pensions preserved or 'frozen' in former employers' schemes, which you will have to claim. The Pensions Advisory Service (OPAS) should be able to help you with this.

 If you have any problems with pensions that you cannot sort out with the pension provider, contact OPAS, 11 Belgrave Road, London SW1V 1RB. Tel: 0171-233 8080.

The Pensions Registry, PO Box 1NN, Newcastle Upon Tyne NE99 1NN. Tel: 0191-225 6437, also provides help with tracing pensions frozen in former employers' schemes.

Pensions and divorce

Women who have seen their husbands' occupational pensions as their main source of retirement income may find their standard of living greatly reduced if they get divorced. Older women divorced shortly before their spouse is due to receive an occupational pension should try to ensure that the value of this important asset is included in any divorce settlement.

Although it is not yet possible to split a pension at the time of divorce, since April 1997 it has been possible for judges to earmark part of the future pension and the lump-sum death benefit for a divorced spouse. Splitting a pension on divorce is likely to become possible within the next few years.

 For more information about all aspects of separation and divorce, including the legal and financial aspects, see Age Concern Books' *Separation and Divorce* (details on p 200).

Personal pensions

Self-employed people and employees who do not belong to a company scheme can take out a personal pension. Employees can contract out of SERPS or opt out of a company scheme to take out an approved personal pension.

Personal pensions work like money-purchase occupational schemes in that your pension is based on a pension fund built up over the years. You can take up to 25 per cent of the fund as a tax-free lump sum and must use the rest to buy a lifetime annuity. You get full tax relief on pension contributions, provided they do not exceed the limits laid down by the Inland Revenue.

Personal pensions are very flexible:

▶ The proportion of your income the Inland Revenue allows you to contribute increases as you get older.

▶ You can choose to draw your pension as early as 50, but you can continue to contribute to a personal pension scheme until you are 75 as long as you are still earning.

▶ You can usually vary your contributions according to your financial circumstances.

▶ The 'open market option' means you do not have to purchase your annuity from your original pension provider. You can shop around among different insurance companies and choose the one that suits you best.

▶ The new rules on 'deferred withdrawal' allow you to take cash from your pension fund without buying an annuity until the age of 75. This means that if annuity rates are very poor when you retire, you can postpone buying one in the hope that rates will improve. However, deferred withdrawal is likely to be worthwhile only for those with a substantial fund – £100,000 or over.

There are various types of personal pension on offer:

UNIT-LINKED POLICIES Your contributions are invested in unit trusts (see p 40) and the value of the fund is directly related to the market performance of the units that are purchased.

WITH-PROFITS POLICIES offer some guaranteed return. Bonuses which cannot be taken away are added during the lifetime of the plan, and usually a variable terminal bonus at the end.

DEPOSIT-BASED PLANS are more like ordinary savings accounts. They make safe havens for people nearing retirement who do not want to take any risk with the fund they have already built up.

If you have dependants, be sure that the whole value of the fund is returned to them if you die before drawing your pension, rather than just the contributions.

Buying an annuity

You must use your pension fund (minus the lump sum) to buy an annuity. How much you get will depend on your age, sex and health, the insurance company chosen, and interest rates at the time of purchase. Insurance companies offer various types of annuity:

FLAT-RATE ANNUITIES, where the income you receive remains fixed from the outset.

ESCALATING ANNUITIES, where the income increases annually to help offset inflation. But you will receive a lower starting income than with a flat-rate annuity, and it will probably be a good many years before you compensate for this difference. If you are not in good health and members of your family do not tend to be long-lived, it may be better to go for a flat-rate annuity.

JOINT SURVIVOR ANNUITIES for husband and wife, where the income is paid until the death of the last survivor.

GUARANTEED PAYMENT ANNUITIES, where the income is guaranteed for five or ten years: if you die before that time, the income is paid into your estate.

For more details about all types of pension, see Age Concern Books annual publication *The Pensions Handbook* (details on p 198).

The State Retirement Pension

To qualify for the State Retirement Pension you must have

▶ reached pension age (60 for women, 65 for men), and

▶ satisfied the National Insurance (NI) contribution conditions (described below).

Your Retirement Pension may consist of a Basic Pension, an Additional Pension and a Graduated Pension. People over 80 who have not paid enough contributions for a Basic Pension may receive a non-contributory pension (£37.35 a week in 1997–98). All elements of the Retirement Pension are taxable.

Parliament has passed legislation to equalise pension age at 65 for both men and women. This is to be phased in over ten years, starting in 2010. No one born before 5 April 1950 will be affected by the change.

FACTFILE

▶ Research commissioned by Age Concern in 1995 suggests that older people need at least £125 a week to achieve a modest lifestyle.

▶ In 1993 only 28 per cent of single pensioners had an income of £125 a week or more.

▶ Only 29 per cent of couples had a joint income of £250 a week or more.

Pensions and other benefits are normally updated on 6 April each year. The new rates are generally announced the preceding autumn.

The Basic Pension

The Basic Pension is paid at the same rate to everyone who has fulfiled the contribution conditions (£62.45 a week for a single person in 1997–98 and £37.35 for a wife on the basis of her husband's contributions, with an extra 25p for people over 80).

INCREASES FOR DEPENDANTS If you are a married man and your wife is under 60 when you draw your pension, you may be able to claim an increase for her as a dependant (£37.35 a week in 1997–98). If your wife receives certain other State benefits or earns more than a certain amount (including any occupational or personal pension), you may not be able to receive this.

If you are a married woman you may be able to claim a similar dependant's increase for your husband, provided you were claiming an increase for him with Incapacity Benefit immediately before you started drawing your pension.

See pages 25–26 for information on Incapacity Benefit.

THE CONTRIBUTION CONDITIONS You will get the full Basic Pension if you have paid, or been credited with, NI contributions for most of your 'working life'.

WORKING LIFE This is the number of tax years during which you are expected to pay, or be credited with, NI contributions. This normally starts in the tax year when you were 16 and ends with the last full tax year before your 60th (women) and 65th (men) birthday.

Age Concern Factsheet 20 *National Insurance contributions and qualifying for a pension* includes information relevant to people whose working life started before 1948, when the present NI scheme began.

QUALIFYING YEAR A tax year in which you have paid, or been credited with, enough contributions to go towards a pension. To be entitled to a full pension, about nine out of every ten years of your working life have to be qualifying years. If you have not got enough qualifying years to qualify for a full pension, you may receive a reduced pension or none at all.

PENSION FORECAST You can find out whether you have paid enough contributions to get a full pension by completing form BR 19, obtainable from your local Benefits Agency (social security) office. Your contribution record may be better than you expect because you have received credits or Home Responsibilities Protection.

CREDITS may be given if you are under pension age and registered for Jobseeker's Allowance; if you are unable to work because you are sick or disabled; if you receive Invalid Care Allowance. Men aged 60–64 who are not paying contributions normally receive credits automatically.

HOME RESPONSIBILITIES PROTECTION (HRP) protects the contribution record of people who cannot work regularly because they have to stay at home to look after a sick or disabled person or children. HRP makes it easier for you to qualify for a full pension: each year of 'home responsibility' will be taken away from the number of qualifying years you need to get a full pension – though it cannot normally be used to reduce the number of qualifying years below 20.

In some circumstances you receive HRP automatically, but sometimes you need to claim it – check the position with the local Benefits Agency (social security) office. HRP does not apply to years before 1978.

LATE OR VOLUNTARY CONTRIBUTIONS You may be able to pay these if there are gaps in your contribution record.

Normally you need to have satisfied the contribution conditions in your own right, but there are the following exceptions:

MARRIED WOMEN of 60 or over who have not paid enough contributions for a pension in their own right can draw the married woman's pension (£37.35 a week in 1997–98) when their husband draws his pension, depending on his contribution record. Any years for which you paid married woman's reduced-rate contributions will not count towards a pension in your own right. (Starting to pay reduced-rate contributions is no longer an option.)

SEPARATED WOMEN who do not qualify for a pension in their own right may be able to claim a married woman's pension on their husband's contributions in the same way.

DIVORCED PEOPLE who do not remarry before pension age and who do not qualify for a full pension in their own right may be able to substitute their former spouse's contribution record for their own, either just for the period of the marriage or from the start of their working life up until the divorce, in order to draw a full Basic Pension. You are not entitled to your former spouse's Graduated or Additional Pension.

WIDOWS who do not remarry before pension age can draw a Basic Pension on their own and/or their husband's contributions. They can also inherit their husband's Additional Pension as well as their own, up to the maximum amount for a single person, and half his Graduated Pension.

If you were aged 55–64 when your husband died, and had not started to receive a Retirement Pension, you can receive a Widow's Pension

(£62.45 a week in 1997–98), depending on your husband's contribution record. You may also receive his Additional Pension, or a pension from his occupational or personal pension scheme. You may also be entitled to Widow's Payment, a non-taxable lump-sum payment of £1,000, paid mainly to widows under the age of 60.

WIDOWERS may be entitled to a Basic Pension on their wife's contributions, plus her Additional Pension (up to the maximum amount for a single person) and half her Graduated Pension, provided they were both over pension age when she died.

Additional Pension

The Additional Pension, paid under the State Earnings-Related Pension Scheme (SERPS), is based on earnings on which you have paid contributions since April 1978. You may qualify for an Additional Pension even if you do not have the minimum number of qualifying years for a Basic Pension.

The Additional Pension is related to weekly earnings between certain levels known as the 'lower and upper earnings limits'. Earnings from past years are revalued in line with increases in average earnings. Your total revalued earnings are then divided by 80 to give the yearly amount of Additional Pension. People reaching pension age after 6 April 1999 will receive less.

If you belong to a 'contracted-out' occupational pension scheme or an approved personal pension scheme, you will not be part of SERPS, as explained on page 9.

Graduated Pension

Graduated Pension is based on contributions on earnings paid between April 1961 and April 1975 (1997–98 figures: women receive 8.11p per week for every £9 of contributions paid, while men receive 8.11p for every £7.50 paid). You can receive Graduated Pension even if you do not qualify for a Basic Pension.

Claiming your pension

About four months before you reach pension age (60 for women, 65 for men) you should receive a claim form. If you do not receive one, write to the local Benefits Agency (social security) office. A married woman claiming a pension on her husband's contributions will need to fill in a separate form. Your pension can be backdated for up to three months if you make a late claim.

You can choose to have your pension paid in two ways:

► by weekly order book which you cash at a post office – however, order books will be phased out during 1997 and 1998 and replaced by benefit payment cards;

► directly into a bank, building society, Girobank or National Savings investment account, paid in arrears either four-weekly or quarterly.

If you think you have been awarded the wrong amount of pension, you can either ask to have the decision reviewed or you can appeal against it.

If you carry on working after pension age

Your State Pension will not be affected by the amount you earn or the number of hours you work. However, if you draw an increase for a dependent husband or wife this may be affected by their earnings, as explained on pages 13–14.

If you lose your job or become unable to work because of ill-health, you will not be able to claim Jobseeker's Allowance or Incapacity Benefit because neither of these benefits can start to be paid to someone over pension age.

Deferring your pension

You can choose to defer drawing your pension for a period of five years in order to earn extra pension. Even if you start drawing your pension you can change your mind and defer it instead – but you can only do this once.

If you defer your pension, it is increased by about 7.5 per cent for each full year that you do not draw it, or 37.5 per cent over the full five years, which would bring the Basic Pension up to about £85.85 a week

(1997–98 figure). Your Additional and Graduated Pension are increased in the same way.

Any weeks in which you defer your pension but claim a Widow's Pension will not count towards extra pension.

EXTRA PENSION FOR MARRIED WOMEN If you are aged 60–64 and entitled to a pension on your husband's contributions, you can defer this to gain an increase. If your husband defers his pension, you will not be able to draw yours until he draws his. Then you will both receive increases. If, while your husband is deferring his pension, you draw another benefit such as Additional Pension or Graduated Pension, your pension on your husband's contributions will not be increased. It may therefore be better not to draw a small Additional or Graduated Pension if your husband is deferring his pension.

FACTFILE

▶ In 1994–95 51 per cent of pensioner households depended on State pensions and benefits for at least 75 per cent of their income.

▶ State Basic Pension for a single person is less than 18 per cent of average adult earnings.

▶ In 1994–95 63 per cent of pensioners received occupational pensions; the median pension received was £43.10 a week (this means that half had a pension of this amount or less and half had a pension of this amount or more).

 For more information on deferring your pension, see Age Concern Factsheet 19 *Your State Pension and carrying on working.*

If you stop working before pension age

If you retire early, you will want to make sure that you qualify for a full pension when you reach pension age. You receive credits automatically if you are receiving a benefit such as Incapacity Benefit or Jobseeker's Allowance (JSA) or if you are a man aged 60–64 – unless you are abroad for more than half the year. If you are under 60 and seeking work, it may be worth registering for JSA even if you are not entitled to benefit because you will then receive credits. If you are not entitled to credits, you may want to pay voluntary contributions.

Although you cannot draw a State Retirement Pension before pension age, there are other benefits you may be able to claim:

JOBSEEKER'S ALLOWANCE This replaced Unemployment Benefit in 1996 for people who are actively seeking work. There are two elements: contribution-based JSA, which is based on your NI contribution record, and income-based JSA, which is means-tested.

Contribution-based JSA can be paid for up to 26 weeks (£49.15 for people aged 25 or over in 1997–98); there are no additions for dependants. This will be reduced if you have an occupational or personal pension of over £50 a week.

Income-based JSA can be paid in addition to contribution-based JSA or on its own after 26 weeks, depending on your income and savings. The rules for calculating benefit are similar to those for Income Support, described on pages 20–21.

INCAPACITY BENEFIT Depending on your contribution record, you may be entitled to this benefit, described on pages 25–26.

INCOME SUPPORT Depending on your income and savings, you may be entitled to Income Support, described on pages 20–21.

HOUSING BENEFIT AND/OR COUNCIL TAX BENEFIT You may be entitled to these benefits, depending on your income and savings (see pp 22–23). You may qualify for some benefit even if you do not qualify for Income Support or income-based JSA.

 Age Concern Books annual publication *Your Rights* (details on p 198) gives full details of the State Pension and other State benefits available to older people.

Benefits for people with low incomes

There are certain State benefits that are available to people whose income and savings are below a certain level. Income Support, Housing Benefit and Council Tax Benefit all help with regular living expenses, while the Social Fund provides lump-sum payments for exceptional expenses. In addition, people with low incomes may be able to get financial help towards such expenses as house repairs and dental care.

If, for example, you leave work before you reach State Pension age and have only got a small occupational pension, it may be worth checking whether you are eligible for any of these benefits.

Income Support

Income Support tops up your income to a weekly level set by the Government. You do not need to have paid NI contributions to qualify. You may receive Income Support if:

▶ You are aged 60 or over or you are under 60 but do not need to register for Jobseeker's Allowance, for example because you are ill or because you are a carer. Unemployed people receive income-based JSA instead.

▶ Your savings are £8,000 or less.

▶ You have a low income.

▶ You are 'habitually resident' in the UK. If you have entered the UK within five years of your claim, you will be asked about this. Contact a local advice agency if this occurs.

To work out whether you qualify you need to:

1 ADD UP THE VALUE OF YOUR SAVINGS If your savings (and capital) are more than £8,000, you will not be eligible. For a couple savings are added together, but the limit is the same. (You will count as a couple whether

you are married or you live with someone as though you were married.) If you have savings between £3,000 and £8,000, an income of £1 per week will be counted for every £250 or part of £250 over £3,000 (this is known as 'tariff income'). Some savings are ignored completely, including the value of your home.

2 ADD UP YOUR INCOME Your income includes earnings, State benefits, occupational and personal pensions, and any tariff income on savings between £3,000 and £8,000. Certain income will be ignored, including Housing Benefit and Council Tax Benefit and actual interest on savings. For a couple, the income of both partners is added together.

3 WORK OUT YOUR APPLICABLE AMOUNT This is the amount per week the Government says you need to live on. It is worked out by adding together the personal allowance (£49.15 for a single person over 25, £77.15 for a couple, in 1997–98) and any premiums that apply to you. Premiums are extra amounts awarded to people over 60, disabled people and carers who are entitled to Invalid Care Allowance (see p 27).

For homeowners mortgage interest and certain other housing costs may be included in your applicable amount (this help may be reduced if an adult 'non-dependant' lives in your home).

4 COMPARE YOUR INCOME WITH YOUR APPLICABLE AMOUNT If your income is less than your applicable amount, you will qualify for Income Support (depending on your savings). If your income is more, you will not get Income Support but you may still get Housing Benefit or Council Tax Benefit.

To claim Income Support, you will need a claim form from the local Benefits Agency (social security) office.

 For more information about how your savings and income affect your entitlement to income-related benefits, see Age Concern Factsheet 16 *Income-related benefits: income and capital.* See also Factsheet 25 *Income Support and the Social Fund.*

£

Housing Benefit and Council Tax Benefit

Housing Benefit basically provides help with rent and certain service charges, for council, housing association or private tenants. The maximum Housing Benefit you can get is 100 per cent of your rent including service charges. If a heating charge is included in your rent this will not be covered. To qualify for Housing Benefit, you must have savings of £16,000 or less and a low income. If you have a partner your combined income and savings will be taken into account, but the limits will be the same.

Council Tax Benefit provides help with paying the Council Tax. There are two types, known as 'main Council Tax Benefit' and 'second adult rebate'. You may qualify for the former if you have savings of £16,000 or less and a low income. The maximum benefit you can get is 100 per cent of your Council Tax. You may get second adult rebate of up to 25 per cent if you have one or more adults with a low income living with you, regardless of your income and savings.

To work out whether you qualify for Housing Benefit or Council Tax Benefit, you follow the same steps as with Income Support (see pp 20–21):

1 ADD UP YOUR SAVINGS, but this time the savings limit is £16,000.

2 ADD UP YOUR INCOME, again including tariff income on your savings.

3 WORK OUT YOUR APPLICABLE AMOUNT, but there are no additions for home-owners' housing costs.

4 COMPARE YOUR INCOME WITH YOUR APPLICABLE AMOUNT If your income is the same as or less than your applicable amount, you will normally get all your rent or Council Tax paid (though a deduction will usually be made if you have an adult 'non-dependant' living with you).

If your income is more than your applicable amount, your benefit will be reduced. You first work out the difference between your income and your applicable amount. Your maximum Housing Benefit is reduced by 65p for every pound that your income is more than your applicable amount, while your maximum Council Tax Benefit is reduced by 20p for every pound.

If you are claiming Income Support or income-based Jobseeker's Allowance, you can fill in a claim form for Housing Benefit and Council Tax Benefit at the same time. If not, you claim directly from your local council.

 For more details about Housing Benefit and Council Tax Benefit, see Age Concern Factsheet 17 *Housing Benefit and Council Tax Benefit.*

Other help with the Council Tax

In addition to Council Tax Benefit, there are various other ways in which your Council Tax bill may be reduced:

EXEMPTIONS Some properties, mainly certain empty ones, are exempt. From April 1997 'granny annexes' are exempt in certain circumstances.

DISABILITY REDUCTION SCHEME Your property may be placed in a lower band if it has certain features which are important for a disabled person. (Properties are all allocated to one of eight bands (A–H) depending on their estimated value.)

DISCOUNTS may be given if you live alone, or if a second person living with you is 'severely mentally impaired' or a carer.

 For more details about Council Tax, see Age Concern Factsheet 21 *The Council Tax and older people.*

The Social Fund

The Social Fund provides lump-sum payments to people with low incomes to help with exceptional expenses. These are mainly available to people on Income Support and income-based Jobseeker's Allowance, but people on Housing Benefit or Council Tax Benefit also qualify for Funeral Payments. Cold Weather Payments and Funeral Payments are mandatory (they must be made if you fulfil the qualifying conditions), while Community Care Grants, Budgeting Loans and Crisis Loans are all discretionary. For people over 60 savings over £1,000 will normally be deducted from any payment; for younger people this applies to savings over £500. Budgeting Loans and Crisis Loans must be paid back, but they are interest-free.

Other help for people with low incomes

If you receive a benefit such as Income Support, income-based Jobseeker's Allowance or Housing Benefit, you may qualify for certain other benefits, including:

GRANTS FOR REPAIRS AND IMPROVEMENTS Local authorities offer three types of grant: renovation grants, home repairs assistance and disabled facilities grants, as described on pages 125–126 and 172–173.

GRANTS FOR INSULATION AND DRAUGHTPROOFING These are available under the Home Energy Efficiency Scheme, as explained on page 127.

HELP WITH FUEL BILLS If you have difficulty paying quarterly bills, you may feel it would be easier to have a prepayment meter installed. If you are on Income Support, you may be able to get a loan or grant from the Social Fund towards the cost of installing one. You may also be able to pay off a fuel debt by going on 'fuel direct': some of your benefit is withheld each week and paid direct to the fuel company. At the time of writing this scheme is being reviewed.

 See pages 127–128 for information on different sources of help with heating and insulation. For more detailed information see Age Concern Factsheet 1 *Help with heating.*

HELP WITH HEALTH COSTS If you receive Income Support or income-based Jobseeker's Allowance, you will be entitled to free prescriptions, dental treatment and eye tests, and help towards glasses. If you do not receive either of these benefits but your savings are no more than £8,000, you can fill in form HC 1 (available from dentist, optician, hospital or Benefits Agency office) to apply for a certificate of low-income entitlement. Certificate HC 2 entitles you to the same amount of help as people on Income Support, while certificate HC 3 entitles you to more limited help. Hearing aids and chiropody services are free to everyone under the NHS, and prescriptions are free if you are over 60, but provision of chiropody services varies.

LEGAL FEES If you are on Income Support or income-based Jobseeker's Allowance or have an income of that level, you may get free legal advice and assistance through the Green Form Scheme. For civil cases in a

Magistrates' Court, a solicitor may be able to represent you under the 'assistance by way of representation' scheme. The qualifying limits are roughly the same as for the Green Form Scheme, with a sliding scale of contributions for those whose income is just above the limit. For other civil cases and some criminal cases, you can apply for Legal Aid – though you may have to pay a contribution towards the cost of your case.

TRAVEL CONCESSIONS are available to older people on most forms of transport, as described on pages 88–91.

Benefits for people with disabilities and their carers

Statutory Sick Pay

If you are an employee paying NI contributions and under pension age, you will probably be entitled to Statutory Sick Pay (SSP) if you are off sick for at least four days in a row. This is payable by your employer for up to 28 weeks; the amount depends on your level of earnings.

If you are not entitled to SSP, because you are self-employed or unemployed, you may be entitled to Incapacity Benefit.

Incapacity Benefit

Incapacity Benefit is paid to people under pension age who are unable to work because of illness or disability. It depends on NI contributions, but is not usually affected by other income or savings.

There are three levels of Incapacity Benefit:

THE SHORT-TERM LOWER RATE is payable for up to 28 weeks to people who are not entitled to SSP (£47.10 in 1997–98).

THE SHORT-TERM HIGHER RATE is paid from 29 to 52 weeks (£55.50 in 1997–98).

THE LONG-TERM RATE is paid after 52 weeks (£62.45 in 1997–98).

The short-term lower rate is not taxable; the other rates are. Additional sums are payable if you become disabled before 45. Increases for adult dependants can be paid only for a husband or wife aged 60 or over, and depend on their earnings.

To qualify for the short-term lower rate you will need to provide a medical certificate stating you are unable to do your usual job. After 28 weeks you will normally have to undertake an 'all-work' incapacity test to decide whether you are capable of doing any work.

If you were receiving Invalidity Benefit on 12 April 1995, you will be covered by transitional rules introduced to protect people from any reduction in the benefit they were receiving. In this case your benefit will not be taxable.

Severe Disablement Allowance

This is a benefit for people who are unable to work because of long-term sickness or disability but have not paid enough contributions to get Incapacity Benefit (basic rate £37.35 a week in 1997–98, plus £22.40 for an adult dependant, depending on their income). There are also additions related to the age at which you became unable to work. You must be under 65 when you first claim.

Disability Living Allowance

Disability Living Allowance (DLA) is for people who become disabled before the age of 65; from October 1997 you must also claim before you reach 65. It does not depend on NI contributions, is not affected by income and savings, will not normally affect other benefits or pensions, and is not taxable. It is intended to help with the costs of being disabled, but you don't have to use it to buy care: it is up to you how you spend it.

DLA has two parts, a care component and a mobility component:

THE CARE COMPONENT is for people who need help with personal care, supervision, or to have someone watching over them. It is paid at three levels (£49.50, £33.10 and £13.15 in 1997–98). People who need help with 'bodily functions' (for example eating, moving around, going to the toilet) or continual supervision during the day and the night receive the higher level; those who need such help during either the day or the night receive the middle level; those who need help for a significant portion of the day get the lower level.

THE MOBILITY COMPONENT is paid at two different levels (£34.60 and £13.15 in 1997–98). People who cannot walk or have great difficulty walking receive the higher level, while people who need someone with them when walking outside receive the lower level.

 For information about the Motability scheme and other concessions for people who receive the mobility component of DLA, see pages 95–96.

Attendance Allowance

Attendance Allowance is for disabled people aged 65 or over. It is paid at two levels: both the rates and the criteria are the same as for the higher and middle levels of the care component of DLA. There is no mobility component.

Invalid Care Allowance

This benefit can be claimed by people under the age of 65 who are unable to work full-time because they care for a severely disabled person for at least 35 hours a week (£37.35 a week in 1997–98, plus £22.35 for an adult dependant, depending on their income).

Invalid Care Allowance (ICA) does not depend on NI contributions, but you cannot receive it if your earnings are over a certain limit or if you receive certain other benefits. The person you look after must receive Attendance Allowance, the higher or middle level of the care component of DLA, or Constant Attendance Allowance. Anyone receiving ICA will automatically receive NI credits towards their State Pension.

 The DSS Benefits Enquiry Line provides information about benefits for disabled people and their families or carers: Freephone 0800 88 22 00 weekdays 8.30am–6.30pm, Saturday 9am–1pm.

 For more details about benefits for people with disabilities, see Age Concern Books annual publication *Your Rights* (details on p 198) or the *Disability Rights Handbook*, available from the Disability Alliance, 1st Floor East, Universal House, 88–94 Wentworth Street, London E1 7SA.

Your tax position

AT A GLANCE

▸ Income Tax

▸ Capital Gains Tax

▸ Inheritance Tax

Under the UK tax system people are assessed annually to determine whether they are liable to pay any tax for that tax year (the tax year runs from 6 April one year to 5 April the following year). There are three main taxes payable by individuals: Income Tax, Capital Gains Tax and Inheritance Tax. While evading tax is against the law, avoiding tax – arranging your affairs so that you pay as little tax as possible – is both legal and sensible. This section gives a brief outline of how the tax system works.

Income Tax

Income Tax is paid on what you earn and on what you receive as a pension or from investments. Your liability for Income Tax (and Capital Gains Tax) is assessed annually by your tax office: your employer's office, if you are still in paid work; your last employer's office, if you are unemployed or retired; the office covering your business, if you are self-employed. If you are self-employed, you are responsible for declaring your earnings to the Inland Revenue. Tax is calculated on the income you receive in the current tax year.

If you are self-employed or a higher-rate taxpayer or receive some untaxed income, you will be sent a tax return each year. Under the system of self-assessment introduced in April 1997, you can choose whether to calculate the amount of tax due yourself or let the Inland Revenue do it. If you want the Inland Revenue to do it, you must send back the completed tax return by 30 September; if you calculate the tax yourself, you have until 31 January to do it.

Since April 1996 all taxpayers are obliged by law to keep records of their income and capital gains.

Calculating your Income Tax

To work out whether you will have to pay Income Tax, or to check that you are paying the correct amount, you need to do the following:

1 ADD TOGETHER ALL YOUR INCOME FOR THE YEAR Some income is tax-free, including certain State benefits for people with disabilities and people on low incomes, and normally the first £30,000 of a redundancy payment.

To add up your total gross income (which you need to do if you want to check that you are paying the right amount of tax), you will need to 'gross up' any income received with tax already deducted. For example, if you received £800 building society interest with tax at 20 per cent deducted, this is equivalent to £1,000 gross income. (All investment income is taxed at 20 per cent for basic-rate taxpayers; higher-rate taxpayers will have to pay more.)

2 FIND OUT WHAT TAX ALLOWANCES YOU ARE ENTITLED TO Everyone has a Personal Allowance (£4,045 in 1997–98), with higher levels for people aged 65 or over. There is also a Married Couple's Allowance (£1,830 in 1997–98), again with higher levels for older people – and you may get other allowances too. These allow you to receive a certain amount of income without paying Income Tax. If your income is less than your allowance(s), you do not pay any tax. You cannot, however, be paid any 'unused' allowance.

If your income is over a certain limit (£15,600 in 1997–98), the higher Personal Allowances are gradually reduced to the level of the basic allowance. The higher Married Couple's Allowances are similarly reduced if your income is over a certain level.

Other tax allowances include Blind Person's Allowance and Widow's Bereavement Allowance. The Married Couple's Allowance and other allowances paid at the same rate are restricted to 15 per cent tax relief, as is tax relief on mortgages up to £30,000 and certain types of maintenance payment. (Tax relief on mortgages will be reduced to 10 per cent from April 1998.) Tax relief is also allowed on personal and occupational pension contributions; certain life assurance policies taken out before 13 March 1984 qualify for 12.5 per cent tax relief.

Tax allowances and rates for the following tax year are announced each November in the Budget.

3 DEDUCT YOUR PERSONAL ALLOWANCE (PLUS BLIND PERSON'S ALLOWANCE) FROM YOUR TOTAL INCOME This gives you the amount of your income on which tax must be paid, known as your 'taxable income'.

4 WORK OUT THE TAX YOU SHOULD PAY Using 1997–98 tax rates, take 20 per cent of your taxable income up to £4,100, 23 per cent of your income from £4,100 to £26,100, and 40 per cent of any income over that amount, and add the three figures together. All investment income is taxed at 20 per cent for basic-rate taxpayers. If you receive a Married Couple's Allowance or other allowance that provides 15 per cent tax relief, calculate 15 per cent of this allowance. Deduct this amount from the tax you are due to pay to give your total tax bill.

> **FACTFILE**
>
> ▶ Two-thirds of older people do not have enough income to pay Income Tax (less than £94 a week for a person aged 65–74 in 1996).
>
> ▶ Only 1.5 per cent of people aged 65 or over are higher-rate taxpayers.

 For more details about calculating your Income Tax, see Age Concern Factsheet 15 *Income Tax and older people.*

How income is taxed

Most income is taxed before you receive it.

EARNINGS AND OCCUPATIONAL PENSION Tax is generally collected through the Pay As You Earn (PAYE) system. Everyone who is taxed under PAYE has a code which enables their employer to deduct the right amount.

STATE PENSION If you get a pension from an ex-employer, your State Pension is normally taxed through PAYE too. Otherwise you should receive a Notice of Assessment if you owe any tax.

PERSONAL PENSION Payments are normally made with basic-rate tax already deducted.

INVESTMENT INCOME This is mostly paid with 20 per cent tax already deducted. If you are a non-taxpayer, or liable for tax only on some of the income, you should be able to reclaim the tax. If you are a higher-rate taxpayer, you will have more tax to pay. Where income is paid gross, as with most National Savings accounts, you normally have to pay any tax that is due in a lump sum.

 For more information about Income Tax and all other aspects of the tax system, see Age Concern Books annual publication *Your Taxes and Savings* (details on p 175).

Cutting down Income Tax

TRANSFERRING INVESTMENTS BETWEEN HUSBAND AND WIFE One partner may be paying tax on investment income while the other is not using up their whole Personal Allowance. Or one may be losing some of their extra age-related Personal Allowance because their total gross income (including investment income) is over the allowable limit, while the other's income is well below it. In such cases transferring some investments to the other partner would save the couple tax.

MARRIED COUPLE'S ALLOWANCE The basic level of the allowance can be split between the couple as they choose. In some circumstances this might affect the overall amount of tax paid. The difference between the basic allowance and the higher allowance for couples over 65 must remain with the husband.

PERSONAL PENSIONS You get full tax relief on contributions, so taking out a personal pension is a good way to lower your tax bill if you are still earning.

BANK AND BUILDING SOCIETY ACCOUNTS Non-taxpayers can now apply to have interest paid gross (that is, before tax is deducted), rather than having to reclaim tax at the end of the financial year.

 For information on tax-free investments, such as TESSAs, National Savings certificates and PEPs, see pages 37–41.

Capital Gains Tax

You may have to pay Capital Gains Tax (CGT) if you sell or give away an asset and you make a profit or the asset has increased in value. An asset is something you own, such as shares, antiques or property. However, not all profits are taxed. A certain amount of profit (£6,500 in 1997–98) is exempt each year, while transfers of assets between husband and wife are not affected. In addition, some items are free of CGT, including:

▶ your only or main private residence (but if you give away or leave your house to someone, they may be liable for CGT when it is sold);

▶ private cars, and personal possessions worth up to £6,000 each;

▶ National Savings certificates and most Government stocks;

▶ proceeds of most life assurance policies.

To calculate CGT, the value of the asset when you acquired it is adjusted for inflation using the Retail Prices Index. The adjusted value of the asset is deducted from the selling price (or its market value if you gave it away or sold it for less than its market value) to give the amount of profit, or 'chargeable gain'. 'Allowable losses' can be set against 'chargeable gains' when calculating whether you have CGT to pay. Any profits over the exempt amount are taxed at Income Tax rates as though they were the top slice of your income.

Inheritance Tax

Inheritance Tax (IHT) may have to be paid on what you leave to your heirs or give away in the seven years before your death. However, IHT is not payable on any assets left to a husband or wife, nor if your estate (plus gifts made over the past seven years, excluding those that are tax-free) is worth less than £215,000 (1997–98 limit), after debts and reasonable funeral expenses have been paid. IHT is payable at 40 per cent on any amount over the limit.

Certain gifts are exempt from IHT, whether or not you survive seven years after making them.

Cutting down IHT

For people who can afford to, the easiest way to avoid your heirs having to pay IHT is to make lifetime gifts early or to keep them within the exemption limits. It is also possible to avoid IHT by putting money into a trust. However, trust law is extremely complicated, so it is wise to take professional advice first.

Your savings and investments

Deciding what to do with your savings is never a straightforward matter. The safest investment may not be the most profitable. You will often get better returns by agreeing to tie your money up for a period of years, but you may need access to at least some of your savings for possible emergencies. In addition to whatever you may have saved over the years, when you retire you may receive part of your pension as a lump sum, and you may decide to invest at least part of this. This section looks at some of the investment options, with the aim of helping you choose those best suited to your particular needs.

Advice and protection for investors

Getting financial advice

Many different experts give advice on money matters, including actuaries, accountants, bank managers, insurance salespeople, solicitors and stockbrokers. Some advisers are 'tied'; these 'appointed representatives' can advise only on the products of the company to which they are tied, and usually receive a commission on what they sell. 'Independent' advisers can in theory choose from the whole marketplace; they may in practice advise on a range of products known to them. They may work on a commission basis or receive a fee from the person to whom they give advice.

Under the Financial Services Act 1986, anyone carrying on investment business (including giving advice) must be authorised to do so, either by the Securities and Investments Board (SIB) or by one of the Self-Regulatory Organisations (SROs) or Recognised Professional Bodies (RPBs).

The Personal Investment Authority (PIA) is the main SRO regulating the activities of independent financial advisers. Others are registered with such bodies as the Law Society or the Institute of Chartered Accountants.

If you want to check what kind of business a financial adviser is authorised to do, you can ring the SIB's Central Register (0171-929 3652).

Since 1 January 1995, the PIA has required advisers selling pension plans and life assurance-based products to follow certain procedures:

DISCLOSURE OF COMMISSION They have to tell you exactly how much commission the salesperson is getting. Companies that do not pay commission to staff must give a comparable figure, taking account of factors such as a proportion of the salesperson's basic salary.

KEY FEATURES They must tell you about the aims, risks and benefits of the product and about charges and expenses.

A PERSONAL ILLUSTRATION This must show projected costs and fund growth based on the customer's personal circumstances.

REASON WHY The adviser must write a letter explaining why the product is right for you.

Making a complaint

If you want to make a complaint, there are several different individuals and organisations you can approach:

► the head of the firm in question;
► the appropriate SRO or RPB;
► the relevant ombudsman (Banking, Building Societies, Corporate Estate Agents, Insurance, Investment, Legal Services, Pensions, PIA);
► the SIB.

Future changes

In May 1997 the Government announced its intention of making major changes in the regulation of all financial services.

Compensation arrangements

The SIB has set up an Investors' Compensation Scheme to cover the collapse of authorised firms. The maximum compensation is 100 per cent of the first £30,000 invested and 90 per cent of the next £20,000. If a building society collapses, compensation is limited to 90 per cent of the first £20,000; the Bank of England's Deposit Protection Scheme also offers 90 per cent of the first £20,000. The Policyholders Protection Act provides protection for individual holders of policies with authorised insurance firms.

 To check the credentials of a financial adviser or firm, or obtain more information about complaints and compensation, contact the SIB, Gavrelle House, 2–14 Bunhill Row, London EC1Y 8RA. Tel: 0171-929 3652.

Banks and building societies

Putting money into a bank or building society account is a very 'safe' form of saving. The capital remains intact and can easily be withdrawn, and you receive interest. The disadvantage is that if you take out the interest as it is paid, you will have left only the money you started with – the value of your savings will not keep up with inflation.

Building societies usually offer a variety of accounts, including:

ORDINARY (OR SHARE) ACCOUNTS offer very low rates of interest but are the most flexible in terms of deposits and withdrawals.

EXTRA-INTEREST ACCOUNTS offer much higher rates of interest but are more restrictive as regards minimum sum deposited and notice of withdrawal.

MONTHLY INCOME ACCOUNTS offer monthly interest on lump sums.

FIXED-TERM ACCOUNTS often offer higher rates of interest to investors who are prepared to keep a lump sum with the society for a fixed period – between one and five years.

TAX-EXEMPT SPECIAL SAVINGS ACCOUNTS (TESSAS) allow people to earn tax-free interest on up to £9,000 invested over five years, provided the capital is not touched during that period.

Banks also offer a variety of accounts:

CURRENT ACCOUNTS often offer different rates of interest for different levels of credit, with transaction charges made only when the account is overdrawn. Overdraft rates are high, with unauthorised overdraft rates higher, but they do vary between banks.

DEPOSIT ACCOUNTS are fairly flexible but returns generally do not match the highest rates paid by building societies.

HIGH-INTEREST CHEQUE ACCOUNTS (HICAS) usually invest your money in the City's money markets. They offer higher rates than ordinary deposit accounts but the minimum investment will be higher. HICAs are also offered by finance companies, merchant banks and fund managers.

MONTHLY INCOME ACCOUNTS, FIXED-TERM ACCOUNTS AND TESSAS are similar to those offered by building societies. Always shop around for the best terms.

GIRO PERSONAL BANKING ACCOUNTS allow you to withdraw money at post offices.

 Moneyfacts is a monthly publication giving interest rates for all financial institutions. It also gives details of overdraft terms. From Laundry Loke, North Walsham, Norfolk NR28 0BD. Tel: 01692 500765.

National Savings

National Savings offers a range of accounts, bonds and certificates, all of which can be bought through post offices.

ORDINARY ACCOUNTS offer the convenience of banking at a post office. Interest rates are low, but the first £70 is tax-free.

INVESTMENT ACCOUNTS offer higher interest but a month's notice is required for all withdrawals.

BONDS The Pensioners Guaranteed Income Bond offers a fixed interest rate (7 per cent gross in 1997), paid monthly, for five years. The FIRST Option Bond sets a guaranteed interest rate annually; Income Bonds offer a monthly income. Children's Bonus Bonds (tax-free; for children under 16) and Capital Bonds offer a guaranteed return over five years. In all cases there are penalties for early withdrawal.

CERTIFICATES offer a guaranteed, tax-free return for five years, with lower rates if certificates are cashed in earlier. After five years they earn the General Extension Rate, but you get a higher rate by cashing them in and buying reinvestment certificates. National Savings supersedes one issue with another at short notice, so it is advisable to buy the latest issue when interest rates are high. Index-linked certificates rise in line with the Retail Prices Index as well as paying interest.

PREMIUM BONDS have more to do with gambling than saving: no interest is paid, but after holding one for three months you become eligible for the monthly prize draw.

Government stocks

Loans to the Government, known as 'gilts', work like this: in return for your money, you get a certificate stating you have bought a certain amount of stock, its name, the gross (pre-tax) rate of interest, and the date of repayment. The Government repays the value of the stock to the holder on the redemption date – the date on the stock.

THE NOMINAL OR PAR VALUE is the price at which the Government promises to buy back the stock. For example, if you buy Treasury 6 per cent 1999, and hold it until 1999, you will receive £100 for every £100 of nominal stock you bought. If you bought the stock for £90 per £100 nominal stock, you will make a gain on your capital. If you bought it for £110, you will make a loss. If you sell before that date, you may get more or less because the market price of the stock depends on the demand for it.

THE RUNNING YIELD is the actual interest you get on a stock, which will depend on what you paid for it. If you buy Treasury 6 per cent 1999 at £90 for each £100 nominal stock, your actual interest will be higher than 6 per cent because it is really interest on £90 rather than £100 ($\frac{100}{90} \times 6 = 6.7$). If you buy it for £110, your actual interest will be lower ($\frac{100}{110} \times 6 = 5.5$).

THE REDEMPTION YIELD is the total yield on a stock if held to redemption (maturity). This includes both the running yield and any gain or loss on the gilt at redemption.

What stocks you buy will depend whether you are more interested in income or in capital gain. You could, for example, buy a high-yielding stock and accept a small capital loss at redemption. If you are a higher-rate taxpayer, it is normally better to buy a low-yielding stock and make a capital gain later, as any capital gain on gilts is tax-free.

Gilts can be bought and sold through banks, some building societies and stockbrokers. Those on the National Savings Stock Register can be bought by post through the Bonds and Stock Office – application forms are available from post offices. The commission on small transactions is less if you buy this way.

Stock Exchange investments

Both 'stocks' and 'shares' are issued by companies in order to raise capital: when you buy shares you are buying a stake in a company; when you buy stocks you are making a loan to the company. Shareholders get part of the company's profits as a dividend; stockholders usually get a fixed-interest return.

Stocks and shares are bought and sold on the Stock Exchange and their prices vary from day to day. The cost of buying and selling has fallen recently, particularly for smaller deals. Many banks or building societies offer cheap dealing services. You pay stamp duty of 0.5 per cent on all share purchases. Remember that the value of stocks and shares can go down as well as up.

 For information about stocks and shares and dealing services suitable for small investors, contact the Stock Exchange, Old Broad Street, London EC2N 1HP. Tel: 0171-588 2355.

Investment trusts

One way of spreading the risk associated with the stock market is to buy into an investment trust. This is itself a 'quoted company', which invests capital in a number of other companies. Some trusts divide shares into 'income shares', which get all the income but have a fixed redemption price, and 'capital shares', which get all the benefit from the capital appreciation of the fund. Most trusts now have schemes for accepting lump sums or monthly payments direct, as well as from brokers.

For useful information about investment trusts, contact the Association of Investment Trust Companies (AITC), Durrant House, 8–13 Chiswell Street, London EC1Y 4YY. Tel: 0171-431 5222. They publish a leaflet called *Buying Shares in Investment Trusts.*

Indirect investments

Unit trusts

Buying unit trusts is generally seen as safer than investing directly in stocks and shares. Unit trusts differ from investment trusts in that you are paying into a pool from which shares are bought by managers rather than buying directly into a quoted company. They should always be thought of as investments to be held for at least three years.

Over 10,000 unit trusts are available to investors: some aim for capital growth, some are intended for income, and some offer a mixture of the two. Unit trusts can be bought with a lump sum or with regular monthly payments. They are sold through newspaper advertisements and by banks, building societies and stockbrokers. You should buy unit trusts only from a member of an SRO or RPB (see pp 34–35).

Other indirect investments

PERSONAL EQUITY PLANS (PEPS) You can invest up to £9,000 per year in a PEP; both dividends and profits will be tax-free. However, PEPs should be thought of as very long-term investments, partly because the initial costs could wipe out any early gains.

INVESTMENT BONDS are single-premium life assurance policies. Your money is invested in a fund of pooled investments, rather like a unit trust, and they provide a tax-free income.

INCOME BONDS give a fixed income and return of your capital after an agreed period.

GROWTH BONDS give a return only when they are cashed in.

Life assurance policies

WHOLE LIFE policies pay out on death whenever that occurs, but they are expensive and often unnecessary.

TERM ASSURANCE is cheaper, and the company pays out only if you die within a specified period.

ENDOWMENT ASSURANCE is a way of saving for a guaranteed payment at the end of a fixed number of years, or earlier if you die before then.

ANNUITIES With 'compulsory annuities', bought with the proceeds of a pension fund, the whole amount received is treated as income for tax purposes. With 'purchased annuities', bought with your own capital, part of the income is regarded as repayment of capital, and this amount is tax-free. For the different types of annuity, see page 12.

 For more about investments of all types, see Age Concern Books annual publication *Your Taxes and Savings* (details on p 198).

New individual savings account

In July 1997 the Government announced its intention of developing a new tax-effective individual savings account, building on experience with TESSAs and PEPs. It will probably become available in 1999.

Boosting your income

AT A GLANCE

▶ Boosting your pension

▶ Using your home as capital

When you have made sure you are claiming all the pensions and benefits you are entitled to, and you are not paying more tax than you should, you may still feel your income is insufficient for your needs. The preceding section contains various suggestions about investing your savings to the best advantage, and the possibilities of earning money in retirement are looked at on pages 76–87. This section looks at ways of increasing your income from pensions and of raising money on the value of your home (if you are 70 or over).

Boosting your pension

Increasing your State Pension

If you have had an interrupted career, check what credits you are entitled to – including HRP, which you may have to claim (see pp 14–15). If there are gaps in your contribution record, you may be able to pay voluntary or late contributions, but check with the Benefits Agency (social security) office first: there is no point in paying extra contributions if you have already met the contribution requirements for a full Basic Pension.

The only other option is to defer drawing your pension, as explained on pages 17–18. It is wise to take advice before doing this: it may be better to draw the pension and invest it – possibly in a personal pension if you are still earning.

Increasing a personal pension

As long as you are still earning, you can continue to contribute to a personal pension until you are 75. You can also take out a new personal pension if you have left your company scheme but are continuing to work, either for a new employer or on a self-employed basis.

CARRY-FORWARD FACILITIES enable you to pay a higher contribution than is normally available for the current year if you paid less than the maximum allowable amounts during the previous seven years.

CARRY-BACK FACILITIES enable you to ask for a contribution paid in the current year to be treated as if it was paid in the previous year – which is helpful if your income was much higher that year.

SINGLE-PREMIUM PERSONAL PENSIONS enable you to pay a single contribution, on which you get full tax relief, and draw the pension and tax-free lump sum immediately, even if you are not yet retiring (provided you are aged 50 or over). Paying single premiums also avoids your having to commit yourself to making regular payments.

DEFERRED WITHDRAWAL, as explained on page 11, gives you the possibility of buying an annuity when rates are relatively favourable.

 For more information about pensions, see Age Concern Books annual publication *The Pensions Handbook* (details on p 198).

Using your home as capital

If, as with many people, most of your lifetime's savings are invested in your home, you may find you can boost your income by raising money against the value of the property while continuing to live in it. But you usually have to be at least 70 before you can do this.

Home income plans

With a home income plan (HIP) you mortgage your property for part of its capital value and use the proceeds to buy a lifetime annuity. A loan of £30,000 will give a woman of 75 about £1,300 net income per year and a man of the same age about £1,850 (1997 estimates). This net income is what is left from the annuity when the interest on the loan has been paid. You will receive at least £200 more if you are a non-taxpayer.

For a couple, the annuity operates until the death of the second partner. The property is then sold, the loan is repaid, and the remainder of the proceeds goes into your estate.

Various factors affect the amount of income you can expect to receive: the older you are, the higher the income you will receive. A woman will receive less income than a man of the same age because she is expected to live longer. A couple will also get less.

You are unlikely to be given more than 65–75 per cent of the property's value. The maximum is generally £30,000, which is currently (1997) the maximum amount on which tax relief on loan interest is allowed. Unlike ordinary mortgages, HIPs still attract tax relief at the full basic rate (23 per cent in 1997–98).

HOW ARE STATE BENEFITS AFFECTED? If you are receiving an income-related benefit such as Income Support or Council Tax Benefit, the income from an HIP could mean that you lose all your benefit. Receiving a lump sum (a maximum of 10 per cent of the loan is allowed by the Inland Revenue) could affect your benefit if it brings your capital over the limit of £8,000 for Income Support or £16,000 for Council Tax Benefit.

Home reversion schemes

Home reversion schemes differ from HIPs in that you actually sell all or part of your home rather than taking out a mortgage on it. You then live in it as a tenant. In return you receive either a lump sum or an income for life. As with HIPs, the older you are the more you receive, as the company will be able to recoup its investment more quickly. The amount you receive will be much less than the market value of your home – usually between a quarter and a half. If you opt for a regular income, a woman of 75 can expect to receive about £2,300 extra annual income from selling three-quarters of the value of a property worth £60,000, with the income guaranteed for a minimum of five years and thereafter payable for life (1997 estimate). A man might receive about £3,000. The advantages of reversion schemes over HIPs are that you can receive the whole amount as a lump sum, and there is no ceiling on the amount of the loan.

Their main disadvantage is that you sell your home for a fixed amount and any appreciation in its value goes to the buyer. With an HIP, you still benefit from any increase in its value. But some new schemes do allow you to benefit. One adjusts the annuity rate according to rises in the value of all the properties in the scheme.

As with HIPs, receiving annuity income or a lump sum may disqualify you from receiving Income Support or Council Tax Benefit.

With HIPs or reversion schemes, always check what the position is if you want to move house in the future.

Loans or mortgages

If you do not feel an HIP or reversion scheme would suit you, you may be able to take out a loan using the value of your home as security.

AN ORDINARY REPAYMENT MORTGAGE The disadvantage is that the repayments are likely to be fairly high.

AN INTEREST-ONLY MORTGAGE Here you pay only interest and the loan is repaid on your death or when you sell the property – though the mortgage can generally be transferred to another suitable property. However, the interest payments could still be fairly high.

A SHARED APPRECIATION MORTGAGE These new schemes enable you to take out a loan against the value of your house either with a fixed lifetime rate of interest or with a zero rate of interest. In return you agree to give up a proportion of any future appreciation in the property's value (the proportion is greater with the zero-interest option). The disadvantage of these schemes is that you have to pay the proportion of appreciation when you sell the house; this could leave you with insufficient capital to buy the alternative property you want.

Tax relief is available on loans only if you are using the money to buy your home; it is not available on loans taken out to pay for home improvements or repairs.

Roll-up loans

With a roll-up loan, an interest-only loan is given against the value of your property but some or all of the interest payments are 'rolled up' and added to the loan debt. Both capital and rolled-up interest are repaid when the property is sold. Normally only a small proportion of the property value is lent.

The danger of such schemes is that the debt can mount up extremely quickly, and the loan debt could even overtake the value of the property.

Most companies stipulate that when the loan debt reaches 60 per cent of the property's value you have to start paying interest. You could then find yourself liable for interest on an enormous loan, and have no option but to sell your house to pay it off.

Investment bond income schemes

In the past people have lost very substantial amounts of money through investment bond income schemes against their property. Insurance companies and independent financial advisers have now been asked by their regulatory bodies not to market such schemes to older people.

 For more details about raising income or capital from your home, see Age Concern Books annual publication *Using Your Home as Capital* (details on p 199).

For details of companies offering HIPs, reversion schemes, shared appreciation mortgages and roll-up loans, see Age Concern Factsheet 12 *Raising income or capital from your home.*

Legal protection

Companies offering HIPs or reversion schemes with annuities are covered by the Financial Services Act: they should therefore be members of the Personal Investment Authority, and their policyholders will be covered by the Policyholders Protection Act. Roll-up loans and reversion schemes based on a lump sum are not covered by the Financial Services Act. Companies offering such schemes are therefore unlikely to have any watchdog body supervising their activities.

In 1991 several of the major companies offering HIPs agreed to operate a new code of practice. Look out for their ship logo signifying the SHIP (Safe Home Income Plans) campaign.

Shopping

So far this chapter has looked at ways of increasing your income – such as making sure you claim all the pensions and benefits you are entitled to and getting the most out of your savings and investments. The other side of the coin is making sure you get value for your money when you come to spend it, whatever you choose to spend it on. This section on shopping doesn't aim to tell you what to buy, but rather to give some pointers as to how to make sure you end up with what you want.

Buying food

There are various factors you will probably consider when deciding where to buy food:

▶ price;

▶ accessibility – is the store in easy walking distance, convenient for public transport or with good car parking available;

▶ variety;

▶ quality.

If price is your first consideration, you will almost certainly do well to get at least some of your shopping at a discount food store such as Locost or Netto, but this may not be particularly convenient and will certainly not provide you with variety.

The big supermarket chains

The big supermarket chains generally stock a very wide variety of goods, usually of good quality. How wide the range will depend on whether you shop at a superstore or a smaller high street store. What they sell can be divided into various categories:

- branded goods;
- own-brand goods – usually cheaper than branded goods;
- sub-brands (their own goods under another name) – for example Sainsbury's 'Classic Cola';
- economy lines for a limited range of basic items (own-brand goods with basic packaging, very cheap, going under names like Economy, No Frills, Basics). These are clearly the supermarket chains' response to the competition from discount food stores.

In some cases you may find you prefer the branded item – there are those who feel that nothing matches Heinz baked beans – but it is always worth trying the cheaper lines.

LOYALTY CARDS Many of the big supermarket chains, including Sainsburys, Tesco and Safeway, offer what are called loyalty cards. These look like credit cards and record what you spend when you shop and award you points accordingly. When your total reaches a certain level, you can claim back a discount on goods and services. The details of the schemes differ – whether there is a minimum purchase before you get points; where you can redeem points; how long you have to wait before you can do so. Common to all the cards is that you get roughly one penny back per pound spent – unless there is a special offer. Sainsburys, for example, offers 'bonus' points on certain items. It's worth getting yourself a loyalty card if the shop you go to anyway has one, but it's not worth travelling any distance to get savings of this sort of level.

DISABLED SHOPPERS Many supermarkets offer 'assisted shopping' – someone to go round the store with you and help if you have difficulty reading labels, reaching things off the shelves or pushing your trolley. If possible, phone the store first to let them know you're coming.

HOME DELIVERY Tesco offers home delivery in some areas. Phone 0345 22 55 33 to find out if this service is available in your area. A firm called Flanagans offers home delivery in some parts of London. Phone 0181-877 8002 for details.

Discount food stores

Chains such as Lo-cost, Kwik Save, Netto and Aldi offer a very limited choice of low-priced, own-brand items, with very plain packaging and a very basic arrangement of goods in the store – sometimes goods are in cardboard boxes. Kwik Save offers a much greater selection than the others. They usually don't accept credit cards. In January 1995 the monthly magazine *Which?*, published by the Consumers' Association, found that you could make significant savings by shopping at these discount shops – up to 10 or 11 per cent. If you have plenty of time but limited money, one option could be to buy some items at a discount store and those that aren't available there at a larger supermarket.

Buying clothes

MAIL ORDER If you don't like trailing round shops and find trying on clothes makes you hot and tired, you could try buying through a mail order catalogue. But you will need to make sure that the system for returning unwanted items is easy (see below), or this method of shopping could turn out to cause more trouble than it saves. When buying clothes you can so easily find that a garment doesn't fit – or that you simply don't like it.

CHARITY SHOPS/NEARLY NEW SHOPS Charity shops are springing up all over the place. Some people can't bear the idea of wearing someone else's clothes, others thoroughly enjoy this method of shopping. One advantage (apart from price) is that you find a tremendous variety of clothes – if you are lucky you might pick up 'designer' clothes that you would never dream of buying new.

FACTORY SHOPS These can be a good place to shop if you have one near you. Clarks, for example, has factory shops at Street (Somerset), Kendal, Doncaster and Croydon, among other places, where you can buy discontinued lines or 'slightly second' shoes for as little as half the normal price. The shop at Street is in fact part of a larger Clarks village, which includes many other factory shops. Shops like this often don't advertise themselves in local papers because people know about them already – though they sometimes advertise on local radio stations. If there is anything like this near you, you will probably find out about it by word of mouth.

Buying electrical goods

When spending perhaps several hundred pounds on a single item, it is a good idea to do some research first. *Which?* often carries special features on particular items, for example washing machines or fridges. Different models are assessed using a wide range of criteria, including price, reliability and energy efficiency. You should be able to look up back numbers in your local library; there is an index for each year telling you what has been covered in each month.

 If you are interested in subscribing to *Which?* (£59 a year in 1997), ring the Consumers' Association on 01992 822 800. *Which?* subscribers can also ring the *Which?* Direct Line for consumer advice, further discussion of 'best buys', etc.

When you go to a showroom, be sure you are well prepared.

▶ Have a clear idea of what you want to buy and what features you need. Explain to the assistant what you want.

▶ Ask about the advantages and disadvantages of a particular model, and ask for a demonstration of any features you don't understand. Make sure your questions are answered – by someone else if the sales assistant doesn't know the answer.

▶ Don't be over-impressed by lots of extra features, which you probably wouldn't use anyway.

You may well be offered a 'free credit' deal. This will be exactly what it says provided you pay the full amount by the due date. Otherwise you are likely to find yourself paying hefty interest.

As far as price is concerned, *Which?* (June 1996) found that the major electrical retailers matched each other closely. In fact you may be more likely to get a bargain from a smaller chain or independent retailer – which often offer free delivery, unlike most of the big chains.

Mail order shopping

Mail order shopping isn't particularly cheap or expensive but it is convenient – you don't have to leave the house and you can pay by instalments. The British Code of Advertising Practice, which covers all mail order adverts, states that goods should arrive within 30 days and that you should be able to return unwanted goods within seven days and get your money back.

As one of the problems with mail order shopping is finding that you don't want what you have ordered, the company's policy on returning unwanted goods is crucial. Questions to ask are:

▶ Is there a free 'returns' service, which allows you to return unwanted s well as faulty goods free of charge? Some companies collect unwanted items from your house; others allow you to post them free of charge using a special 'returns' label, which means you don't have to reclaim the cost of postage and packing.

▶ How long have you got in which to return unwanted goods?

Shoppers' rights

Under the Sale and Supply of Goods Act 1994, goods must be of 'satisfactory quality' and fit for the purpose they are sold for – durable, safe, free from minor defects. You must exercise your rights within a 'reasonable' time – but what is reasonable will depend on the facts of the case and the type of goods.

Faulty goods

If something breaks that you've bought very recently, you should be able to get a cash refund or exchange provided you have the receipt. Don't accept an exchange, credit note or repair if you want a refund.

If a product wears out or breaks within an unreasonably short period of time, you can claim compensation on the grounds that it is not of 'satisfactory' quality, but how long something has to work is not defined. If you are not satisfied, it is worth standing your ground.

SALE GOODS You have the same rights with sale goods as with any others: notices that there are 'no refunds on sale goods' do not affect your statutory right to buy goods of a satisfactory quality.

SECONDS If you buy goods labelled as 'seconds', you will still be able to return them if they have faults other than those disclosed when you bought them.

MAIL ORDER Buying mail order gives you just the same protection as shopping any other way.

USING A CREDIT CARD If you pay by credit card, you can claim against the card issuer as well as the retailer for items that cost over £100.

HIRE PURCHASE If you buy goods on hire purchase, your claim will be against the finance company and not the retailer.

How to complain

▶ Be clear about the problem.

▶ Keep your receipt.

▶ Decide whether you want a refund, exchange or repair.

▶ Return the goods as soon as possible. Ring the shop if the item is too big to return.

▶ Visit the shop and speak to the manager.

▶ Follow up your complaint in writing.

▶ Write to the head office if necessary.

▶ If you are still dissatisfied, seek advice from a consumers advice centre, CAB or trading standards department. All local authorities – metropolitan or London boroughs, county councils or unitary authorities – will have a trading standards department.

▶ If you can't settle a dispute with a retailer directly, you could consider going to the small claims court (the sheriff court in Scotland). The procedure is cheap and easy to use and you don't need a lawyer to present your case. If the amount you are claiming is £3,000 or less (£750 in Scotland), your case can be counted as a small claim.

 If you want help in preparing your case, you can go to the CAB or the local authority trading standards department.

A subscription to the Consumers' Association *Which?* Personal Services (£31 a year in 1997) gives you unlimited telephone legal advice. Ring 0645 123 580 for further information.

Unwanted goods

Retailers don't legally have to accept goods back simply because you have changed your mind, although many will give a refund if you have a receipt – some stores set a time limit, for example seven or ten days; others set no limit. Refunds may not be available with certain items such as jewellery, cosmetics and underwear. If you have any doubt at all about what you are buying:

▶ Keep the receipt.

▶ Check before buying if the shop will give refunds and whether there is a time limit for bringing things back.

If you have lost the receipt, other proof of purchase such as a credit or debit card transaction voucher should be accepted. Many shops will give a credit note or exchange without a receipt, but you won't usually get a refund without one.

Paying fuel bills

Most fuel suppliers offer a variety of different ways of paying your bills.

The largest savings are often achieved if you agree to pay by monthly direct debit, but as you save a proportion of the standard tariff the arrangement is most beneficial to those with large bills. With British Gas's DirectPay, for example, you can save up to 6 per cent off the standard tariff; with London Electricity's scheme you save up to 4 per cent.

The disadvantage of paying by direct debit is that you may find that you are paying more or less per month than you need. If you have been paying too little, you could find yourself with an unexpected extra bill to pay at the end of the year. If you have been paying too much, you will get the money back but you might have preferred to have it to spend earlier.

If your fuel bills are fairly modest, you may find another option gives you similar savings. With British Gas's Option Pay, for example, you can save £8 per year simply by paying your quarterly bills within ten days of the issue date.

For information about 'fuel direct', prepayment meters and other options for people who are having difficulties with their fuel bills, see page 24.

Making a Will

Many people never make a Will, yet it is the only way to ensure that your assets are disposed of as you wish after your death. It also makes things much easier for whoever has to sort out your affairs. Anyone over the age of 18 can make a Will, provided they have 'testamentary capacity' – in other words if they fully understand what they are doing.

How to make a Will

Most agencies advise going to a solicitor even with a simple Will, but you can make your Will yourself. Preprinted Will forms can be bought from stationers very cheaply. If you do make your own Will, make sure you:

▶ say that this Will revokes all others (even if you have never made a Will before);

▶ decide who will be your executor – the person named in the Will to administer your affairs after your death;

▶ choose who will be the main beneficiary of your estate – the person (or people) who will receive the remainder or residue of your estate after any specific bequests have been made;

▶ make provision in case any beneficiary dies before you do.

It is a good idea to choose two executors in case one dies before you. People normally choose their spouse or children, but you can choose a professional such as a solicitor or bank manager. The Public Trustee can be appointed if there is absolutely no one else available. Executors can be beneficiaries of the estate.

 For leaflets explaining the role and charges of the Public Trustee, contact The Acceptance Officer, Public Trust Office, Trust Division, Stewart House, 24 Kingsway, London WC2B 6JX. Tel: 0171-644 7000.

Your signature to the Will must be witnessed by two independent people (not your spouse or anyone who stands to inherit or their spouse).

You can keep your Will at home or it can be lodged with a solicitor or bank (banks may charge for this service). The main thing is to make sure that all concerned know where to find it.

 For further information about making a Will see Age Concern Factsheet 7 *Making your Will.*

Going to a solicitor

It is advisable to go to a solicitor unless your Will is very simple, especially if you intend to leave significant sums to people other than those who might expect to inherit, such as your spouse and children. If you do not already have a solicitor, the Citizens Advice Bureau (CAB) may be able to help you find one. The public library may have a directory listing solicitors by area. It is a good idea to ask at the outset what the cost will be.

FACTFILE

▶ It is estimated that about 70 per cent of adults in England have not made a Will.

▶ Dying intestate could in certain circumstances mean your spouse having to sell the home you shared.

If you are over 70 or physically or mentally disabled, and have a low income and little savings, you may qualify for help with making your Will under the Green Form Scheme.

 You will be able to get a list of solicitors in your area who work under the Green Form Scheme either from the local CAB or from the Law Society, 113 Chancery Lane, London WC2A 1PL. Tel: 0171-242 1222.

Financial institutions such as banks, building societies and insurance companies can now prepare Wills as well as solicitors. There are also Will-writing services available, such as that offered by Age Concern England.

Dying intestate

If you die without making a Will – known as dying intestate – your estate will be distributed to members of your family according to certain rules: a husband or wife will receive at least the first £125,000, but surviving children or grandchildren will receive some of the estate if it exceeds £125,000. If you are not married, your parents or nearest relatives will inherit.

Revising your Will

If you marry or remarry, your Will automatically becomes invalid and should be revised (unless you were intending to marry when the Will was made and it refers to your proposed marriage). Codicils (supplements to a Will) can be added to an existing Will for minor changes. For major changes you should make a new Will revoking the former one. Alterations should never be made on the original document.

Other arrangements to be made in the event of death

If you have strong feelings about the arrangements for your funeral – burial or cremation, type of ceremony, etc – you can leave written instructions with your Will.

Funerals are expensive. If you want to ensure that enough money is readily available to cover the cost, this can be done by means of a special bank or building society account, a life assurance policy or a prepayment plan. The National Association of Funeral Directors and Age Concern England offer prepayment plans, as do some friendly societies and a few insurance companies.

 For more information about prepayment plans contact the National Association of Funeral Directors, 618 Warwick Road, Solihull B91 1AA. Tel: 0121-711 1343, or Age Concern England.

 See Age Concern Factsheet 27 *Arranging a funeral* for a list of organisations that offer prepayment plans.

There are certain personal papers that whoever sorts out another person's affairs after their death will need to find. It is a good idea, therefore, if such papers are kept together. Apart from the Will, these include:

▶ details of pensions, insurance policies, investments, bank and building society accounts, credit agreements, credit cards;

▶ property deeds, lease, mortgage details, rent book;

▶ addresses of tax office and professional advisers.

 For more about leaving your affairs in order, see Age Concern England's leaflet *Instructions for My Next of Kin and Executors upon My Death.*

Managing another person's money

A T A GLANCE

▶ If the person is mentally competent

▶ If the person is mentally incapable

You may at some point find you have to take over the management of someone else's money – perhaps that of a parent or other older relative – either permanently or temporarily. In some circumstances you may be asked for help, for example if the other person goes into hospital or needs help with a specific legal transaction such as buying or selling a house. But you might sometimes have to take over without consent, for example if the other person suffers from dementia or a severe form of mental illness.

If the person is mentally competent

Informal arrangements

There are several informal arrangements that can be made by people who are still mentally competent who would like someone else to act on their behalf. Any such arrangement automatically becomes invalid if the person whose affairs you are handling becomes mentally incapable of understanding the arrangement.

THIRD PARTY MANDATE Someone who is physically unable to get to the bank or building society may authorise you to use their account. This is known as a 'third party mandate'.

OPENING A JOINT ACCOUNT This gives you easy access to the funds held in the account. For anyone who opens a joint account with someone other than their spouse, it is advisable to have a written agreement signed by all the account-holders confirming their intentions.

ACTING AS AN AGENT If you collect a social security benefit or pension from the post office on behalf of another person (the 'claimant'), you are acting as their 'agent'. If the arrangement is a temporary one, claimant and agent simply complete the form on the back of the order. If you are likely to be acting as agent for a long time, you can get an agency card from the Benefits Agency.

Appointing an attorney

If someone (the donor) wishes to make more formal arrangements for another person (the attorney) to act on their behalf, he or she can make a power of attorney. A power of attorney provides you with a legal document which proves you are authorised to act on the donor's behalf and shows the extent of your powers.

A power of attorney can be made by anyone who is mentally capable of understanding what they are doing. Donors can appoint anyone they choose to be their attorney. This does not affect their right to act for themselves as long as they remain mentally capable.

There are two main types of power of attorney:

► an ordinary power of attorney;

► an enduring power of attorney.

Both of these can be either general, giving the attorney 'blanket' powers to act on the donor's behalf, or limited to specific powers, for example to buy or sell a house. If the power is to be limited rather than general, it needs to be carefully worded, preferably in consultation with a solicitor.

An enduring power of attorney (EPA)

An EPA is a form of deed which enables donors, while still mentally capable, to appoint an attorney either to take over their affairs at once and to continue to act as attorney if they become mentally incapable or to take over their affairs when they are no longer mentally capable of acting for themselves. An EPA made after 31 July 1991 must be in a form prescribed by law. The form may be purchased from a law stationer or drawn up by a solicitor.

It is advisable to appoint more than one attorney to act jointly and severally (which means that they may act together or separately, as they choose). If the attorneys can only act jointly, it will mean that on the death or incapacity of one of the two the EPA will expire. If only one attorney is appointed and something happens to that person, the donor may not be able to create a fresh EPA.

If you are acting as an attorney under an enduring power, you have a duty to register the power with the Public Trust Office once you consider that the donor is beginning to lose the mental capacity to manage alone.

When trying to decide when someone is 'mentally incapable', you should always assume they are capable until they demonstrate otherwise, for example by consistently losing money and failing to pay bills. People with diagnosed mental health problems such as schizophrenia may be temporarily incapable of managing their affairs. If in doubt, always ask for an opinion from the family doctor.

 For further information and advice about enduring powers of attorney and how to register them, contact the Customer Service Unit (Mental Health), Protection Division, Public Trust Office, Stewart House, 24 Kingsway, London WC2B 6JX. Tel: 0171-664 7000.

If the person is mentally incapable

Unless an enduring power of attorney has been made, none of the arrangements described so far will remain legally valid if the person you are acting for becomes mentally incapable of understanding what is going on. There are various formal arrangements that can be made in these circumstances. Often this will involve applying to the Court of Protection to take over the person's financial affairs, but if the person you want to act for has limited income and savings this may not be necessary.

CLAIMING BENEFITS AND PENSIONS AS APPOINTEE The DSS can appoint another person (the appointee) to collect a social security benefit or pension on someone else's (the claimant's) behalf and to spend it on their needs. A close relative who lives with or visits the claimant frequently will usually be preferred. If the claimant has made a power of attorney, the attorney should be appointed.

COLLECTING OTHER PENSIONS OR PAYMENTS Similar arrangements can sometimes be made for an appointee to collect and spend a pension or other work-related payment, for example from a government department or the armed forces.

COLLECTING TAX REFUNDS Tax refunds below a certain amount may sometimes be paid to the next of kin of people who are mentally incapable of managing their own affairs.

USING SOMEONE ELSE'S BANK OR BUILDING SOCIETY ACCOUNT may be possible, for example to make withdrawals to provide for their immediate needs, if they have only a small amount of savings. If the bank or building society refuses, you can apply to the Court of Protection to use the account.

The Court of Protection and the Public Trust Office

The Court of Protection looks after the financial affairs of people who, because of 'mental disorder', are unable to manage for themselves. It refers to these people as 'patients'. The Protection Division of the Public Trust Office is responsible for the day-to-day administration of cases under the jurisdiction of the Court of Protection and for registering enduring powers of attorney. Someone else can be authorised to manage a patient's financial affairs in one of three ways:

▶ The Public Trust Office can register an enduring power of attorney, as described above.

▶ The Court of Protection can appoint a receiver, usually a close friend or relative, to deal with the day-to-day management of the patient's financial affairs. A professional adviser such as a solicitor or accountant can be appointed, but they will usually charge a fee. Overseeing the administration of the receivership is then the responsibility of the Public Trustee.

▶ The Public Trustee can issue an order authorising a patient's assets to be used in a certain way for his or her benefit (provided the patient's affairs are straightforward and their income is small and savings less than £5,000).

If the patient's affairs are not straightforward, even if the savings amount to less than £5,000, an application should be made to the Court of Protection to appoint a receiver.

 For more about all aspects of managing other people's money see Age Concern Books' *Managing Other People's Money* (details on p 199) or Age Concern Factsheet 22 *Legal arrangements for managing financial affairs.*

Using your time

- ▶ Educational opportunities
- ▶ Community involvement
- ▶ Earning money in retirement
- ▶ Travel
- ▶ Going on holiday

When you retire, all the time previously occupied by work – including travelling, and perhaps doing extra in the evening – is yours to spend as you choose.

People retiring in the 1990s can expect to spend nearly as long in retirement as they did at work. Retirement can amount to one-third of your life or more. The very word 'retirement' is becoming an anachronism: nowadays the term 'third age' is increasingly used.

The fact that you have so much time at your disposal over so long a period makes it all the more crucial to make good use of it. In this period of life many people discover talents and skills they never knew they had.

Educational opportunities

You may wish to study for your own personal satisfaction or in order to learn a specific skill that will increase your earning potential. You may want to study informally or you may hope to take examinations and gain qualifications. You may see going to a class largely as a way of meeting congenial people. Whatever you are hoping to get out of further study, there are a great many opportunities open to people who want to learn in retirement.

Informal ways of learning

RADIO AND TELEVISION At the most informal end of the spectrum, many radio and television programmes are in the widest sense educational, and many specifically educational programmes are broadcast, sometimes at night, often accompanied by cassettes, videos and books. This is a particularly good way of learning a language. For those with cable TV, the Learning Channel offers a range of informative programmes while the Discovery Channel focuses largely on different parts of the world and nature programmes.

SCIENCE ON CHANNEL FOUR If you would like answers to any questions relating to science, engineering, technology, medicine or health, phone Science Line on 0345 600 444, open weekdays 1–7 pm. **Science Line** offers access to 1,000 scientists across the country and has close links with major museums. A subscription to **Science Line Up** gives you six newsletters a year, a countrywide guide to science-related events and other benefits. If you have access to the Internet, you could try visiting **Science Net**, Channel Four's 'one-stop science site'.

THE INTERNET If you have access to the Internet (lowest subscription about £6 per month in 1997 – or try your local library), you can try 'surfing' on the World Wide Web (www). Key in a couple of words to indicate what you're looking for and see what a 'search engine' (such as Lycos or Yahoo) comes up with. The 'web' is best at providing information on topical subjects. One snag is that it can get very congested and slow: the morning is probably the best time to try it (before the Americans get up).

LOCAL LIBRARIES may run their own activities. They are increasingly setting up 'open learning' centres where you can learn to use computers; they have various learning programmes, sometimes including the Internet.

MUSEUMS AND GALLERIES In addition to visiting a museum or gallery, you may find that the education department provides a programme of courses, lectures and events for interested adults.

 If you would like advance information on programmes and publications of particular interest to you, you could take out a subscription to Channel Four Select. Write to them at PO Box 4000, London W5 2GH. For details of Channel Four educational programmes, contact Channel Four Learning, Castle House, 75–76 Wells Street, London W1P 3RE. Tel: 0171-580 8181.

Ring BBC Education on 0181-746 1111 for information on language courses and other educational programmes.

For answers to queries arising from any programme on Home and Leisure or Discovery Channel, ring their Viewer Relations Department on 0171-462 3600.

ScienceNet's web address is http://www.campus.bt.com/CampusWorld/pub/ScienceNet/

If you are starting something completely new, you may like to join the Dark Horse Venture. Their philosophy: it's never too late to start from scratch. To join you have to be 55 or over and take up an activity you have never tried before. Awards are given to people for meeting the targets they have set themselves. There are no exams and no comparisons: your personal best is what you aim for.

 For more information about the Dark Horse Venture, contact them at Kelton, Woodlands Road, Liverpool L17 0AN. Tel: 0151-729 0092.

Attending classes locally

One of the easiest ways of extending your education in retirement is to go to a class near your home.

LOCAL AUTHORITY ADULT EDUCATION SERVICES usually offer a wide variety of classes, academic, vocational, physical and practical. English literature, computer studies, keep-fit and cake decorating are examples. Some lead to recognised qualifications. Prospectuses should be available mid-August. Fees vary, but there are generally reductions for pensioners.

WORKERS' EDUCATIONAL ASSOCIATION (WEA) classes tend to be more academic than those run by local authorities. There are more than 1,000 branches in Great Britain – you can obtain the address of your local branch from the library or local authority education office.

UNIVERSITY OF THE THIRD AGE (U3A) The term 'university' is misleading: no qualifications or exams are involved. People join U3A groups to study a wide range of topics, not all of them academic. All activities are arranged by the members themselves. At a national level U3A publishes a termly newspaper called *Third Age News* and runs a travel club.

THE NATIONAL ADULT SCHOOL ORGANISATION organises local study groups which meet in members' homes or other premises, weekly or fortnightly. It publishes a monthly magazine, *One and All*.

THE PRE-RETIREMENT ASSOCIATION (PRA) promotes the development of courses and materials for pre-retirement education. The national office is the centre of a network of local PRA groups.

WEA, 17 Victoria Park Square, Bethnal Green, London E2 9PB.
Tel: 8181-983 1515.

U3A National Office, 26 Harrison Street, London WC1H 8JG. Tel: 0171-837 8838 – send a large sae for a list of addresses of local U3A groups.

National Adult School Organisation, MASU Centre, Gaywood Croft, Cregoe Street, Birmingham B15 2ED. Tel: 0121-622 3400.

Pre-Retirement Association of Great Britain and Northern Ireland, 26 Frederick Sanger Road, Surrey Research Park, Surrey GU2 5YD. Tel: 01483 301170.

 For information and ideas about sporting activities, see pages 134–138.

Finding out what's available

MANY LOCAL AUTHORITIES offer educational guidance services for adults where you can discuss your particular needs and find out what's available locally.

LOCAL LIBRARIES will have information about what is provided by the local authority and local interest groups.

YOUR LOCAL AGE CONCERN GROUP should be able to give you information. Many run their own learning programme.

THE AGE CONCERN EDUCATION AND LEISURE NEWSLETTER, produced three times a year, is available on request from the Education and Leisure Officer at Age Concern England. There is also a series of free *Education and Leisure Activity Guides*.

AGE RESOURCE, the younger arm of Age Concern, will give advance information about courses, events and activities of all sorts for people aged 50 or over in different parts of England.

TRAINING ACCESS POINTS (TAPS) give information about training and leisure opportunities in your area. Ask at your local library if there is a TAP near you.

Phone Age Resource on 0181-679 2201 to find out if there is an Age Resource Desk near you. They will tell you the person to contact and opening hours. If there isn't a Desk near you, they will give you information on your area.

Learning away from home

If you do not want to commit yourself to an ongoing course, short residential courses are a useful alternative, provided you can afford the fees. Intensive courses like this can be a good way of obtaining a measure of expertise relatively quickly.

SUMMER SCHOOLS, run by universities and some independent boarding schools, notably Millfield and Taunton schools in Somerset, offer study holidays for all ages. Grandparents and grandchildren can go together.

FACTFILE

▶ People are retiring earlier and living longer.

▶ In 1994 less than 51 per cent of men aged 60–64 worked; 69 per cent of women aged 55–59 worked.

▶ A man aged 60 can expect to live another 18 years, and a woman of the same age another 22 years.

RESIDENTIAL STUDY BREAKS are offered by all kinds of colleges, schools and field study centres. Many people come on their own to these courses, so a study break is one solution to the problem of holidaying on your own experienced by many single people.

 For information about summer schools send for a copy of the *Summer Schools Supplement* from the Independent Schools Information Service, 56 Buckingham Gate, London SW1E 6AG. Tel: 0171-630 8793 (cost £1.50), or *Summer Academy Study Holidays* from Summer Academy, Keynes College, The University, Canterbury, Kent CT2 7NP. Tel: 01227 470402.

For more information about residential study breaks, see *Time to Learn*, published twice a year by the National Institute of Adult Continuing Education, 21 De Montfort Street, Leicester LE1 7GE. Tel: 0116 255 1451.

 For information about study breaks, contact British University Accommodation Consortium, Box 1504, University Park, Nottingham NG7 2RD. Tel: 0115 950 4571.

Distance learning

'Distance learning' refers to learning by post, radio, television or electronic mail, or by using a distance learning package. The term 'open learning' implies flexibility as regards the content and duration of courses: you can decide what you learn and over what period of time. All the main providers of distance learning courses have a high proportion of older students.

THE OPEN UNIVERSITY offers courses and study packs on a vast range of subjects – arts, sciences, social sciences, community education and leisure, among others – in addition to its degree courses (see below).

THE OPEN COLLEGE OF THE ARTS aims to provide home-based education in a wide range of arts subjects, including music, photography, creative writing, garden design and art history. You may also be required to attend occasional tutorials at a regional study centre.

THE NATIONAL EXTENSION COLLEGE (NEC) offers a wide variety of courses, from maths and electronics to birdwatching, counselling and business skills, including courses specifically geared to the needs of people who left school without qualifications and have not studied for some time.

THE OPEN COLLEGE provides flexible vocational training, with home-based courses, plus access to special equipment such as computers and laboratories through a number of centres.

In addition, colleges offering correspondence courses are widely advertised in newspapers and magazines.

 For more information about OU courses, contact the Open University, Central Enquiry Service, PO Box 200, Milton Keynes MK7 6YZ. Tel: 01908 653231. Or you can visit one of its 13 regional centres for information and advice.

Open College of the Arts, FREEPOST, Barnsley S70 6BR. Tel: 01226 730495.

NEC, 18 Brooklands Avenue, Cambridge CB2 2HN. Tel: 01223 316644.

Open College, FREEPOST, Warrington WA2 7BR.

For general information on correspondence courses, or to check the credentials of a correspondence college, contact the Council for the Accreditation of Correspondence Colleges, 27 Marylebone Road, London NW1 5JS. Tel: 0171-935 5391.

For further information see the *Open Learning Directory*, published by Pergamon, available at most reference libraries.

Taking a degree

Most universities accept mature students for degree courses on the basis of their experience rather than the paper qualifications demanded of school-leavers. If you have not taken a degree before, you may be eligible for a grant from your local authority to cover tuition fees.

The Open University (OU) has no admission qualifications, but OU students do not qualify for ordinary local authority grants. There may, however, be other help available, as explained in their booklet on financial support.

An OU degree will normally take between four and six years. You acquire credits on completion of a course: you need six credits for a BA, eight for a BA Honours degree. Degrees can be made up of various combinations of courses.

 For a list of useful addresses and publications, see Age Concern Factsheet 30 *Leisure education.*

See page 77 for suggestions about further training, for those interested in earning some money in retirement.

Community involvement

Working people often admit they really haven't a clue about what goes on in the neighbourhood they live in – which is not surprising if they regularly leave for work before eight and don't return home until six or seven in the evening. Becoming more involved in the life of the local community can be extremely rewarding; it can also greatly ease the transition from full-time work to retirement.

Joining a club or society

The best source of information is your local library, where you will find leaflets and notices on a wide variety of clubs and societies. Before committing yourself to join, you should be able to have a look at a copy of their forthcoming programme and attend an initial meeting as a guest. This will give you an idea of the level at which the society is pitched and of what the atmosphere is like.

Joining a society or club is one way of taking a hobby or interest a bit further, and at the same time meeting people with similar interests to yourself. If you enjoy painting or photography, you could join an art society or photography club. For those who are keen to go back to their roots, family history societies exist all over the country. A keen gardener might join the local horticultural society. If you enjoy scrabble, chess or bridge, you could join a local club, even enter competitions.

Clubs for older people

Large employers such as the civil service and National Health Service and some big companies run clubs for former employees. If you are fit and active and have just retired, the idea of joining a club whose members are largely much older than you may not seem very appealing – and this is likely to be equally true of local Age Concern groups.

However, it might be worth getting their newsletter: the club may have more to offer than you expect. An increasing number of local Age Concern groups now offer leisure programmes. The activities of Age Concern Leicester, for example, include a writers' group, painting and drawing, keep fit, dancing, indoor bowls and bingo. They also run classes in conjunction with the local further education institute. In addition, active retired people with a bit of time to spare are always needed as volunteers – to help organise activities and perhaps to visit housebound members.

Women's clubs

If the name Women's Institute (WI) conjures up for you a picture of jam-making and apple pies, you may be pleasantly surprised: their talks and discussions cover a great variety of topics, and they offer a wide range of courses, including running a small business and computer studies. The WI has branches in town and country alike, as does the Townswomen's Guild, with over 2,000 branches.

 For information about your nearest WI branch, contact the National Federation of Women's Institutes, 104 New Kings Road, London SW6 4LY. Tel: 0171-371 9300.

For the address of your nearest Townswomen's Guild branch, contact the Townswomen's Guild, Chamber of Commerce House, 75 Harbourne Road, Edgbaston, Birmingham B15 3DA. Tel: 0121-456 3435.

Companionship organisations

For many single people, the biggest barrier to enjoying leisure activities or trying something new is the lack of a companion. This applies particularly to older women, as there are substantially more older women than men. Solitaire – Friends Indeed and Single Again are organisations set up specially to offer a solution to this problem. Members all receive introductions to other members in their area. There are also organisations that exist to find people a companion to go on holiday with – see pages 100–101.

 Solitaire – Friends Indeed, 82 Main Road, Hockley, Essex SS5 4RF. Tel: 01702 204154.

Single Again, Suite 33, 10 Barley Mow Passage, London W4 4PH.
Tel: 0181-749 3745.

If you enjoy the theatre but don't have anyone to go with, the Theatregoers' Club of Great Britain arranges trips for its members. It has 80 branches, mainly in the south-east of England in easy reach of London's West End.

For men, joining one of the clubs for ex-service personnel run by the Royal British Legion and other ex-service organisations can be another good way of meeting people.

 For the address and phone number of your local booking secretary, contact the Theatregoers' Club of Great Britain, Harling House, 47–51 Gt Suffolk Street, London SE1 0BS. Tel: 0171-450 4040.

Joining an environmental group

Many people spend the bulk of their working lives indoors and see retirement as an opportunity to redress the balance. Joining a group such as Friends of the Earth, the Ramblers' Association or the Royal Society for the Protection of Birds combines outdoor activities and a positive commitment to protecting the environment. The Ramblers, for example, go on regular walks, at the same time keeping footpaths open and preserving people's right of access to the countryside.

The British Trust for Conservation Volunteers has 750 local groups in rural and urban areas throughout the country. They teach and practise skills such as coppicing, hedging and drystone walling. They also organise working holidays.

 To find out your nearest group, contact British Trust for Conservation Volunteers, 36 St Mary's Street, Wallingford, Oxon OX10 0EU. Tel: 01491 839766.

Working as a volunteer

If you have time and energy to spare, working as a volunteer can be extremely satisfying. It can enable you to put the skills you have acquired while working to good use. Alternatively, it can give you the chance to do something completely different from your pre-retirement job, and perhaps to develop new skills. If you miss working with other people, it can help fill this gap in your life too.

The opportunities for doing voluntary work are endless. You could do work for your church or for a political organisation. As already mentioned, you could help organise outings and other activities for a club or society you belong to. But you are most likely to find voluntary work with a voluntary agency. Voluntary agencies range from national charities such as Oxfam and Age Concern and campaigning bodies such as Friends of the Earth to community groups and local action groups.

The following examples give some idea of the range of work you can do as a volunteer. You could:

▶ act as a guide or steward in a museum or stately home – the National Trust relies heavily on volunteers;

▶ work as a counsellor for organisations such as the Samaritans, victim support schemes or Relate (formerly the National Marriage Guidance Council);

▶ work with children and young people in a baby clinic, playgroup, youth club, or scouts or guides group;

▶ work with elderly people, helping with shopping or gardening, or perhaps helping in a day centre or residential home;

▶ work in a charity shop.

You could also consider public service work, for example:

▶ becoming a magistrate or local councillor;

▶ sitting on a tribunal, for example a Disability Appeals Tribunal, Social Security Appeals Tribunal or industrial tribunal;

▶ sitting on other public bodies such as the Community Health Council or school governing body.

When considering what would suit you, bear in mind that you have your experience of life to offer as well as the expertise you acquired at work. People who have themselves suffered a bereavement may make good bereavement counsellors; retired people are often more acceptable as counsellors and helpers to people in their own age group simply because they have shared similar experiences.

Some voluntary agencies, such as the Citizens Advice Bureaux, the Samaritans and Relate, are prepared to train volunteers.

How to find voluntary work

If you have already been taking part in some voluntary activity, retirement may simply provide the opportunity to become more involved. If you haven't, there are various places to go for information about vacancies for volunteers in your area.

AGE RESOURCE (see p 66) will be able to give you details of opportunities for all types of voluntary work in your area. A particularly good time to find out about opportunities is during Age Resource Week, run in May each year. Age Resource offers annual national and regional awards to projects that use the skills and experience of older people in a particularly imaginative way.

THE LOCAL LIBRARY will often have leaflets and notices from agencies seeking volunteers. Most reference libraries will have a copy of the *Voluntary Agencies Directory*, published by NCVO Publications, which lists almost 2,500 voluntary agencies. A list of voluntary agencies in your area may be available from the library, the CAB, or the Council for Voluntary Service (CVS) or Rural Community Council.

THE VOLUNTEER BUREAU Check in the local telephone directory to see if there is one in your area.

REACH, the Retired Executives Action Clearing House, specialises in finding part-time expenses-only jobs with voluntary agencies for retired professional and business men and women.

THE RETIRED SENIOR VOLUNTEER PROGRAMME (RSVP) Volunteers work together as a team on local community projects.

THE NCVO AND THE NATIONAL CENTRE FOR VOLUNTEERING both publish information leaflets about employment opportunities, paid and unpaid, in the voluntary sector.

VOLUNTEER FAIRS are held in many areas during Volunteer Week in May each year. Organisations needing help set out their stall and try to attract people to offer their services.

THE NATIONAL VOLUNTEERING HELPLINE Phone 0345 22 11 33 (weekdays 10 am–4 pm) to find out what has been registered with them in your area.

For details of Age Resource awards, and to find out if there is an Age Resource Desk in your area, contact Age Resource at Astral House, 1268 London Road, London SW16 4ER. Tel: 0181-679 2201. If there isn't a Desk near you, they will give you information themselves.

To find where your nearest CVS is, contact the National Association for Councils for Voluntary Service (NACVS), 3rd Floor, Arundel Court, 177 Arundel Street, Sheffield S1 2NU. Tel: 0114-278 6636. For your nearest Rural Community Council, contact Action with Communities in Rural England (ACRE), Somerford Court, Somerford Road, Cirencester, Glos GL7 1TW. Tel: 01285 653477.

To find out if there is a Volunteer Bureau in your area, contact the National Association of Volunteer Bureaux, New Oxford House, 16 Waterloo Street, Birmingham B2 5UG. Tel: 0121-633 4555.

If you are interested in a REACH placement, contact REACH, Bear Wharf, 27 Bankside, London SE1 9ET. Tel: 0171-928 0452.

To find out whether RSVP has a group in your area, contact RSVP, 237 Pentonville Road, London N1 9NJ. Tel: 0171-278 6601.

For more about working as a volunteer, and for many constructive suggestions about using your time, see Age Concern Books publications *Changing Direction* and *An Active Retirement* (details on pp 200–201). Age Concern Factsheet 31 *Older workers* includes many useful addresses and suggestions for further reading.

For an information leaflet contact either the NCVO (National Council for Voluntary Organisations), Regent's Wharf, 8 All Saints Street, London N1 9RL. Tel: 0171-713 6161 or the National Centre for Volunteering, Carriage Row, 183 Eversholt Street, London NW1 1BU. Tel: 0171-388 9888.

Earning money in retirement

AT A GLANCE

▶ What could you do?

▶ Working for someone else

▶ Working for yourself

Before deciding to take on any paid work, it is worth having a good look both at your financial position and at what you are hoping to get out of retirement. How much money will you need, both in the immediate future and in the years ahead? You may feel you would rather reduce your expenditure in some way than give up any of your precious leisure time. On the other hand, developing an existing hobby or interest further could also turn out to be a good way of earning some extra money. And if you want to take up an expensive hobby such as photography, you may not be able to do so at all without some extra income.

What could you do?

What have you got to offer?

When you first ask yourself the question 'What do I have to offer?' you will probably think of the skills associated with your pre-retirement job. If you don't want to carry on doing the same sort of job, or even working in the same field, you may feel you are at a dead end. But in order to answer the question properly, you need to take a far broader look at yourself and what you can do. It is vital to look at all the possibilities. Here are some other questions you might ask yourself:

WHAT SPECIAL SKILLS OR KNOWLEDGE HAVE I GOT? In addition to the skills directly related to your job, you are likely to have some more general skills such as an ability to communicate well with other people or a good head for figures. It can be a useful exercise to make a list of all the skills you possess. To do this properly you will need to cast your mind over all the different areas and stages of your life.

HAVE I GOT HOBBIES OR POSSESSIONS WITH EARNING POTENTIAL? If you enjoy decorating, for example, you could start doing it for other people. If you have a computer, you could go into desktop publishing. You can also hire the equipment you intend to put to money-making use.

What about further training?

Further training could enable you to change direction completely. In addition to the various educational opportunities discussed on pages 63–69, you may be eligible for Government-funded Training for Work if you are under 64 and have been signing on as unemployed for at least 26 weeks. Ask about this at the local Jobcentre.

A variety of training opportunities are provided by 81 local Training and Enterprise Councils (TECs) through many different training organisations (Local Enterprise Councils (LECs) play the same role in Scotland). TECs/LECs are privately run, so what is on offer will vary from area to area, but they should all offer advice about courses and getting financial support.

One way of financing training is to take out a Career Development Loan; phone 0800 585 505 for details or ask at your local Jobcentre or TEC/LEC.

If what you really want is recognition of your existing skills, you could put yourself on a crash course and gain a professional qualification. Although National Vocational Qualifications (NVQs) are generally achieved in the workplace and based on your experience at work, it is possible to obtain one at a college, by means of work experience gained there. Another new option is Accreditation of Prior Learning: you put together a portfolio of past work experience that shows that you've already reached the level of competence required for an NVQ.

 Training Access Points (TAPs) give information about training and leisure opportunities in your area. Ask at your local library if there is a TAP near you.

Another possible source of advice and information is Third Age Challenge Trust (TACT), Anglia House, 115 Commercial Road, Swindon SN1 5PL. Tel: 01793 533370. TACT helps set up work and training projects for older people.

Teletext 630 'Jobs and Courses' on Channel 4 gives suggestions about training opportunities.

For the address and phone number of your local TEC/LEC, contact the local Jobcentre.

Where to go for help

You may get help in thinking through the options from:

▶ a client adviser at the local Jobcentre;

▶ your local TEC/LEC;

▶ the local authority careers service – many authorities offer adult careers guidance;

▶ private companies offering careers guidance, but it can be expensive – always check first to make sure that what they are offering is really what you want;

▶ books at your local library.

Working for someone else

Although many retired people feel attracted by the idea of becoming self-employed, many still prefer the greater security and more reliable income associated with working for someone else.

WORKING PART-TIME The majority of people who earn money in retirement work part-time. Although part-timers are not usually paid at a lower rate than people working full-time doing the same job, part-time jobs may be less interesting and involve less responsibility than full-time jobs.

JOB-SHARING provides a kind of halfway house between full-time and part-time work: two or more people share the hours, duties, pay and benefits of one full-time job.

TELEWORKING You can work at home for an employer, keeping in touch with employer and customers through computers, telephones and faxes (many teleworkers are self-employed).

Where to look for a job

There are various sources from which post-retirement jobs may be sought:

JOBCENTRES run by the Employment Service. A client adviser will talk to you about the kind of work you want, advise you on benefits and help you draw up a Jobseeker's Agreement. This will set out what type of work you are looking for, what steps you will take to find work and what help the Jobcentre will give you; it will be reviewed regularly. After 13 weeks you may be able to attend a Jobsearch Plus course, which will provide practical help with job-hunting, preparing a CV, and interview techniques. After six months you will get a Restart interview; you may be able to go to a Jobclub or undertake Training for Work.You may also be offered an interview through the Job Interview Guarantee scheme or a three-week Work Trial without coming off benefit. Further interviews and courses are offered after one year and two years.

 The leaflet *Just the Job*, available from Jobcentres, explains what help the Jobcentre can offer.

EMPLOYMENT AGENCIES Apart from the many ordinary employment agencies you will find listed in the *Yellow Pages*, there are a number that specialise in finding jobs for retired or older people. These include Age Works, the Over 50s Employment Bureau, Careers Continued and Forties People (the last two cover London only). Some local Age Concern groups have established their own employment agencies. There are also several agencies that specialise in recruiting staff for charities.

 For the names and addresses of employment agencies for older people, and of other useful organisations, see Age Concern Factsheet 31 *Older workers* or Age Concern Books publications *Changing Direction* and *Earning Money in Retirement* (details on pp 199–200). Both of these include a sample CV and covering letter.

NATIONAL AND LOCAL PRESS, RADIO AND TELEVISION Some national newspapers advertise different categories of job on different days. It is also worth looking in professional and trade journals: the Classified Index of *Willings Press Guide* gives details of all such journals published in the UK. Some local radio stations advertise job vacancies.

NETWORKS 'Networking' refers to the use of contacts to obtain advice, information and jobs. The 'old boy system', clubs and professional associations are examples of networks. Less formally, your network may include your family, neighbours and friends, and people you meet through your church, your trade union or your local pub.

SELF-ADVERTISING Advertisements in the national or local press, putting a notice in a shop window, and writing to prospective employers telling them what you can offer are all forms of self-advertising. If you write to employers it is always worth sending a curriculum vitae or CV (see pp 81–82).

Combating ageism

You may find that some employers hold negative misconceptions about the potential of older people. Will you be in poor health? Will you be able to retrain? Will it be worth offering training if you are unlikely to continue working for long? Will you be willing to work under a less experienced and perhaps less qualified supervisor? These are some of the questions employers may ask if you are over 50. As a result employers may refuse to consider applicants purely on age grounds, without considering what they have to offer, or else offer ridiculously low salaries.

FACTFILE

▶ Men's levels of economic activity declined for all age groups between 1971 and 1996. The fall was sharpest for men aged about 55–65.

▶ Women in general became more economically active over the same period, with a very small decline at around 60.

▶ In 1994 more than a quarter of the UK workforce were working part-time and the proportion is increasing.

Fortunately attitudes are changing: many larger employers are realising the benefits of employing older workers and making it a priority to recruit more people over 50. You should nevertheless be aware that negative stereotypes may exist. If you want to get a job, you may need to point out the falsity of such views and to emphasise the positive aspects of age, including:

▶ a lifetime of experience;

▶ reliability and proven ability;

▶ availability and flexibility.

 Too Old . . . who says? published by the Department for Education and Employment, contains useful advice for older workers. It is available from Jobcentres and TECs/LECs.

Preparing your CV

A curriculum vitae or CV is your personal advertisement, giving details of your education, qualifications and previous employment. When you apply for a job you may well be asked to send a CV but it is usually a good idea to send one anyway.

A good starting point is to take two or three pieces of paper and write down information under the following headings:

PERSONAL DETAILS Your date of birth, marital status, address, etc.

EMPLOYMENT HISTORY Details of the jobs you have had, working backwards (ie giving your last job first): the years when you started and left each job; the name, address and business of each employer; your job title. You may in fact decide to leave out some of your earlier employment history if it does not seem relevant or if you have had a great many jobs.

SPECIAL EXPERIENCE OR ABILITIES Type of work done for previous employers; the types of equipment you used; your salary; your responsibilities; promotions achieved; number of people supervised. You may not want to include all this information in your final CV, but it is useful to gather it all together at this stage.

EDUCATION AND QUALIFICATIONS Educational institutions attended, starting with your secondary school, and qualifications obtained (but if you have higher educational qualifications, it may not be necessary to include the lower school ones). Include any vocational training you have done.

OTHER INFORMATION Anything else you think might be relevant, such as hobbies, proficiency in languages, voluntary activities, clean driving licence.

How you present your CV is almost as important as what is in it. It is therefore vital that it should be typed and well laid out. The advantage of doing it on a word processor is that any number of good copies can be produced, and information can easily be added or deleted. This makes it easy to make adjustments to your CV, emphasising the experience that is most relevant to a particular job vacancy.

Jobclubs and the various courses on offer at Jobcentres give help with producing a CV.

Choosing referees

You should also think of possible referees at this stage. Normally two will be sufficient. A former employer will probably be able to give information on your ability to do the job, and whether you will fit into the existing workforce, while a person of some standing such as a clergyman or doctor who has known you for a considerable time will be able to vouch for your character.

You do not need to include names of referees in your CV, but it is advisable to get their agreement and have names and addresses ready so that you can supply them without delay if asked.

The covering letter

Unless your CV is accompanying a job application form, you will also need to write a covering letter. This should be brief but positive. This is particularly important if you are writing to prospective employers on your own initiative rather than applying for an advertised vacancy.

It is usually advisable to state the type of work you are prepared to accept: you may need to make clear that you are not necessarily looking for a post equal in status to your pre-retirement job.

Preparing for an interview

It may be many years since you were last interviewed for a job. Some reminders about how to prepare for an interview may therefore be useful. Your preparation will consist mainly of gathering background information and thinking about questions you might be asked.

BACKGROUND INFORMATION Information about your prospective employer – what the company does or makes, how many people it employs, who its main customers or clients are, and so on – can be obtained from people you know who work for the company, or for its competitors; the Department of Employment; trade directories; or, in the case of a public company, the *Stock Exchange Year Book*, available in most local libraries.

QUESTIONS YOU MAY BE ASKED Apart from the general questions often asked at employment interviews such as 'Why do you want this job?', you are likely to be asked questions specifically relating to your age such as

'What is your health like?' and 'What have you done to keep up to date in your field?' (see p 80). Because of the negative stereotypes held by some employers, it is particularly important to have answers prepared to questions such as these. What you have that younger people won't have is experience, so make the most of that.

THE GOING RATE FOR THE JOB You may also be asked what rate of pay you expect. In this case it is as well to know the 'going rate'. You can obtain information about current wage rates from people working in similar occupations; job advertisements for similar work; employment agencies or trade unions; or the annual New Earnings Survey issued by the Department of Employment, available in most reference libraries (but this is always out of date, so you will need to add increases for inflation).

Working for yourself

'Setting up your own business' can encompass anything from doing some dressmaking or decorating for friends and neighbours to running a shop or working as a management consultant.

Offering a service

Offering some sort of service on a freelance basis can be an ideal way of continuing to earn some money when you have retired. If you enjoyed your pre-retirement job, you might like to carry on doing the same sort of work. Alternatively you might prefer to develop a hobby or leisure interest into a money-making activity.

Consultancy

Another possibility is to become a consultant – someone who is approached by others for advice and assistance because of his or her knowledge, skill or expertise. You can set yourself up as a consultant in almost any field – fashion, computers, tax, even retirement. You should, however, make sure that you keep up to date with developments in your field and that you comply with all regulations relating to a particular field of activity. Independent financial advisers (or consultants) must, for example, be authorised by a regulatory body such as the Personal Investment Authority (PIA).

What should you charge?

If you are self-employed, deciding how much to charge for your services is always difficult. You will not want to price yourself out of the market, nor to sell yourself ridiculously cheap.

Some professional bodies such as the Law Society or the accountancy bodies issue guidance on fees and charges. Apart from this, one way of fixing fees is simply to charge 'what the market will bear', or what a prospective client is willing and able to pay. Another is to do a costing exercise. Costs basically comprise three items:

▶ materials;

▶ labour costs (what you consider a fair rate for the type of work you do);

▶ overheads – advertising, depreciation, heating and lighting, telephone, stationery, etc.

A rough-and-ready method is to add a fixed percentage for overheads, say 75 per cent, to your labour rate. If your labour rate is £10 an hour, a 75 per cent overhead of £7.50 will give you a total hourly rate of £17.50.

Buying an existing business

You can find out what businesses of the type you want are available through the appropriate trade journal or a business transfer agency (look in your local *Yellow Pages*).

Once you have found a business that seems suitable, you should try to discover as much as you can about it. Apart from anything else you will want to find out what the location is like, what reputation the business has in the area, and why the present owner wants to sell.

When you get to the stage of serious negotiation, it is wise to seek professional help. Briefly, the price you are asked to pay will be determined by four factors:

PROFITS You will need to look at the trend of profits rather than just the absolute level: a business with steadily increasing profits will obviously be worth more than one where profits are declining.

FIXED ASSETS Are the premises freehold or leasehold, and what condition are they in? Are equipment, fixtures and fittings up to date and in good condition?

CURRENT ASSETS The most important current assets are debtors and stock. As far as stock is concerned, an important figure is rate of turnover. Apart from its obvious bearing on profits, this indicates how well the stock carried meets customer requirements.

GOODWILL The value of the connections of an established business.

Starting from scratch

One advantage of starting a business from scratch is that you will not run the risk of being taken in by someone trying to dispose of a business for dubious reasons. You may also need less capital because you will not have to pay for intangible assets such as goodwill. An obvious disadvantage, especially for an older person, is that it may take some time for the business to become viable. In general, the more personalised the product or service you are selling, the more likely it is that you will decide to start from scratch.

Whatever your idea, you need to ask yourself whether you have the necessary skills – research, marketing, selling, bookkeeping, planning, dealing with people – the stamina and the capital. Will you be able to cope with the insecurity and the hard work? Talk to people in the field, read books, go on a course (go to a TAP to find out what is on offer in your area; see p 77).

Buying a franchise

A franchise is the grant of a licence by one person (the franchiser) to another (the franchisee) which entitles the franchisee to trade under the franchiser's name. The franchisee also receives help with establishing and running the business. Franchises on offer in the UK include such household names as the Body Shop, Clark's Shoes and Burger King, as well as many smaller, recently established ones.

One advantage of a franchise is that you are likely to have fewer start-up problems. The disadvantage is that the initial fee can be very large, on top of what you have to pay for premises, equipment, stock, etc. You also have to pay royalties to the franchiser.

 An information pack and a checklist of 50 questions to put to a prospective franchiser are available from the British Franchise Association, Thames View, Newtown Road, Henley on Thames, Oxon RG9 1HG. Tel: 01491 578049.

Where can you go for help?

The most obvious sources of help and advice are your own bank manager, solicitor and accountant. Other local sources of help include TECs/LECs, Chambers of Commerce and Local Enterprise Agencies.

What the Government mainly offers is advice and training. TECs/LECs offer training, advice and support. What is on offer will vary from area to area, but you should be allocated a business counsellor for the first couple of years, who will help you draw up a business plan. The TEC/LEC may be able to offer some start-up funding (under different names in different areas) and/or training vouchers to cover the cost of suitable training. Your business counsellor should be able to advise on other sources of financial help. Check whether you need to take out any special business insurance.

 For details of your nearest TEC/LEC or Local Enterprise Agency, contact your local Jobcentre.

Obtaining self-employed tax status

If the Inland Revenue regards you as self-employed, expenditure you incur in the course of earning your income may be allowed against tax. If you are classed as an employee, you can claim for only a very few items of expenditure. Being classed as self-employed can therefore save substantial amounts of money.

If you set up a business and wish to claim you are self-employed, you should arrange an interview with your local tax inspector. He or she will apply a number of criteria in deciding on your claim:

▶ Do your earnings derive from one source or several? If from only one source, you will have more difficulty in persuading the tax inspector you are self-employed.

▶ How much control do you exercise over what you do and when you do it? If you work regular hours and receive specific instructions on how to do the work, you are likely to be regarded as an employee.

If you are dissatisfied with the tax inspector's decision, you can appeal against it.

 For more information about Income Tax and your tax allowances, see pages 28–33 of this book or Age Concern Books annual publication *Your Taxes and Savings* (details on p 198).

You may also need to start paying Class 2 National Insurance contributions. Check with your local Benefits Agency (social security) office.

Travel

Retired people usually have less disposable income than people in work, but they also have more time. This means they are able to get about more cheaply – and usually more pleasantly – by travelling at off-peak times and taking advantage of travel bargains. Considerable fare reductions are also available to older people on a number of different types of transport.

Concessionary travel

Local buses

In most areas of the country people over pension age qualify for some form of concessionary bus fare. Broadly there are four types of scheme:

▶ travel tokens of a set value which can be used for full or part payment of fares;

▶ passes giving a flat-rate fare for any length of journey on one bus in a given area;

▶ half-fare passes, usually limited to off-peak, weekend and public holiday journeys;

▶ free passes, again usually limited to off-peak, weekend and public holiday journeys.

In Greater London people over pension age qualify for free travel on bus and underground services (9am–3pm weekdays and all day weekends and bank holidays) and on local rail services (after 9am or 9.30am). Apply to your local authority for details for your area.

Trains

A Senior Railcard, available to anyone over 60 (£16 in 1997), gives reductions of one-third on most train journeys. Holders of a Senior Railcard can also buy a Rail Europ Senior Card for £5, which gives savings of up to 30 per cent on rail and sea travel in over 25 countries, including most of western Europe.

The Disabled Persons Railcard (£14 in 1997) offers similar discounts to the Senior Railcard but gives you the option of taking a companion with you at the same reduced rate. The privatisation of British Rail may affect these railcards.

APEX fares, available on a limited number of journeys, also offer considerable reductions over the standard fares, but usually not as great as those available to Railcard holders. In addition, APEX tickets have to be booked seven days in advance and the time of travel cannot be changed. You can get an even greater reduction if a Super Apex ticket is available, but these must be booked 14 days in advance and are very limited in number.

 For details about the Senior Railcard and an application form, see the leaflet *Senior Railcard*, available from most stations and rail-appointed travel agents. For details of the Network Card for use in the London and South-East area, obtain a leaflet from any station in London or the south-east.

Check with the train operator if you need to reserve seats: this is now compulsory for some services and usually advisable for long journeys. Remember it is always more expensive to travel on Friday (and on Saturday in July and August).

CROSSING LONDON For many people the thought of crossing London from one mainline railway station to another presents a major hurdle, but it may in fact be possible to avoid this. The Thameslink Brighton–Bedford line connects various stations south of London with Luton and Bedford. There are also some through trains from the south coast to Midlands and northern destinations, and services from the Midlands to the south via Reading instead of London. The journey may take slightly longer than taking the ordinary services in and out of London, but if you are not in a hurry you may feel it's worth it. There is also a Stationlink bus service that runs between most of the major London terminals.

Coaches

National Express, along with its Scottish partner Scottish City Link, offers discounts of around 30 per cent on most standard fares for holders of the Advantage 50 Discount Coach Card (£8 a year in 1997), available to anyone over 50. Local coach operators may also offer concessions. Look in the *Yellow Pages* under 'Bus and coach services'.

For most services you will need to book in advance, but there are some, such as the Oxford–London service, where you simply pay the driver as you get on. As with trains, travelling on Friday (and on Saturday in July and August) is more expensive. It is always worth keeping an eye open for special offers.

If you are considering travelling by coach, it is worth checking where the pick-up points are. You will not necessarily have to start or end your journey at a coach station.

FACTFILE

► People aged 60 or over travel on average 76 miles per week, compared to 186 miles for men and 126 miles for women in the 16–59 age group.

► The proportion of people aged 65 or over who use public transport fell from 69 per cent to 59 per cent between 1980 and 1984.

► A Consumers' Association survey in 1996 found that one in ten rail customers were being overcharged.

Air

Some airlines do offer reduced fares for older people, but these may not be the cheapest fares available. The cheapest fares are usually the ones with most restrictions and need to be booked well in advance, such as APEX fares. A number of conditions often apply to these fares:

► The outward and return journeys have to be booked and paid for at the same time.

► No alterations are permitted unless a higher fare is paid, and there is little or no refund if you cancel.

► They are only available on certain days of the week or times of the year, and there is a minimum and maximum length of stay.

Cheap tickets are often bought through so-called 'bucket shops', which buy them in bulk from the airlines. It is also worth looking for advertisements in national and local papers. You can travel free on British Airways flights if you ever manage to collect enough 'Air Miles', acquired through purchasing goods and services from the many shops and suppliers participating in the scheme. A return trip to Paris, for example, needs 450 Air Miles.

 For details of the Air Miles scheme phone 01293 513633.

Sea

Some ferry operators offer discounts to Senior Railcard holders, and others offer concessions to passengers above a certain age.

Channel Tunnel

Eurostar offers a Senior Fare for people aged 60 or over. This offers large reductions on the standard fare but may still be more expensive than special offers such as a day return or a Saturday night stopover – though the Senior Fare will be much more flexible. Always check exactly what is on offer before booking.

Travelling for fun

If you have time to spare, it can be enjoyable to travel around for its own sake rather than simply as a means of getting from one place to another. If you haven't got a car, you could try one of the various rover tickets on offer.

ROVER TICKETS can be bought from most major bus companies in the provinces. They give you unlimited travel for a day in their area. One-day travel passes will give you unlimited travel within London.

TOURIST TRAIL PASSES are available from National Express. They give you unlimited travel for different periods, eg for five days' travel within a ten-day period, with extra discounts for Discount Card holders.

COACH TRIPS – days out to sporting events, stately homes and so on – are organised by many coach companies. Companies also provide group travel for clubs and societies of all kinds.

COMMUNITY MINIBUSES exist in many areas, run by Community Transport groups for other voluntary organisations. They do not usually put on transport for individuals, but a group of older people getting together for an outing should be able to hire a minibus quite cheaply.

 To find out about Community Transport groups in your area, contact the Community Transport Association, Highbank, Halton Street, Hyde, Cheshire SK14 2NY. Tel: 0161-351 1475.

 If you are responsible for organising group outings, send for a free copy of *Coaches Welcome* to C W Circulation, Lewis Productions Ltd, Thames Chambers, 2 Clarence Street, Kingston upon Thames, Surrey KT1 1NG. Tel: 0181-481 2000. The booklet contains a county-by-county guide to museums, stately homes, theme parks, etc.

Travel for people with disabilities

Buses

Some operators now use vehicles that meet some or all of the DPTAC (Disabled Persons Transport Advisory Committee) standards, including low steps, visible handrails and easy-to-push bells. A few bus services, such as the Mobility Buses in London and other cities, are accessible to people in wheelchairs.

 For more information on London's Mobility Buses, contact London Regional Transport, Unit for Disabled Passengers, 172 Buckingham Palace Road, London SW1W 9TN. Tel/Textphone: 0171-918 3312.

Trains

Most InterCity stations are easily accessible to wheelchairs, but facilities and availability of staff vary widely. Many smaller stations are unstaffed. Facilities on trains also vary widely. In older trains people in wheelchairs may have to travel in the guard's van, and the toilets will probably not be wheelchair-accessible.

To find out what facilities are available on a particular journey, you should phone the train operator before you travel. They can advise you on the most suitable trains and stations to use, and provide assistance at the departure and arrival stations.

If you need to change trains in London, there is a Stationlink bus service that runs between most of the major London terminals. There is also an Airbus service from Victoria, Euston and Paddington to Heathrow Airport, and a Gatwick Express train from Victoria to Gatwick Airport. All these are accessible to wheelchairs.

 See the leaflet *Rail Travel and Disabled Travellers*, free from main railway stations, for advice and contact addresses and telephone numbers.

Coaches

Again you will need to ask the coach company about facilities at both ends of the journey and on the coach. Coaches cannot usually carry wheelchairs, but National Express is currently introducing a new type of coach which is easier to get on and off.

Air and sea

Air transport has recently become much easier for people with disabilities, but it is always wise to phone the airline or airport first to check what facilities are available and whether any special arrangements need to be made. The same is true if you are travelling by sea.

Door-to-door transport

If you are disabled and cannot use ordinary public transport, and do not have access to a car, there are a number of door-to-door transport schemes you may be able to use. Charges are usually much lower than for an ordinary taxi.

SOCIAL CARS Under social car schemes people volunteer to use their own cars to drive people who cannot use public transport. Drivers receive expenses, and you contribute a non-profit fare – usually more than a bus fare but less than for a taxi. Ask at your local library or CAB about schemes in your area. Schemes are often run by the local Volunteer

Bureau, Council for Voluntary Service (CVS) or Rural Community Council. Some are run by the British Red Cross or the Women's Royal Voluntary Service (WRVS).

 See p 75 for details of how to find out the address of your nearest CVS, Rural Community Council or Volunteer Bureau.

DIAL-A-RIDES Dial-a-ride schemes use converted cars or minibuses with pull-out steps, ramps or passenger lifts. Schemes exist all over the country under a variety of names: some will take you anywhere within their area, others concentrate on a few selected destinations. They will usually not take you to hospital as this would undermine the ambulance service. Most schemes want you to register with them, and to book your journey in advance. Some charge will be made. Ask at the local library, CAB, Council for Voluntary Service (CVS) or Rural Community Council for details of local schemes, or try the local authority transport planning department or social services department.

 The Department of Transport's Mobility Unit has a database listing of community transport schemes by county. They will print out and send you the section relating to your area. Available from Mobility Unit, Zone 1/11, Great Minster House, 76 Marsham Street, London SW1P 4DR. Tel: 0171-271 5252. Textphone: 0171-271 5252.

 For free telephone advice and information for elderly and disabled people about any aspect of travel or transport, contact Tripscope on 0345 58 56 41.

TAXICARD SCHEMES These enable disabled people in Greater London to use taxis at greatly reduced fares. Barnet, Redbridge and Westminster run their own schemes; no scheme is currently available in Greenwich or Lambeth.

 To find out if there is any concessionary scheme operating in your area, contact your local council, or London Regional Transport, Unit for Disabled Passengers, 172 Buckingham Palace Road, London SW1W 9TN. Tel/Textphone: 0171-918 3312, if you live in London.

Cars

For many people with disabilities a car is the only suitable form of transport, and having a car greatly increases their independence. If you are thinking of buying a car, there are various sorts of help available.

INFORMATION AND ADVICE Both the Mobility Advice and Vehicle Information Service (MAVIS) and the Mobility Information Service (MIS) offer information and advice to disabled drivers.

MAVIS, Department of Transport, TRL, Crowthorne, Berkshire RG45 6AU. Tel: 01344 661000.

MIS, National Mobility Centre, Unit 2a, Atcham Industrial Estate, Shrewsbury SY4 4UG. Tel: 01743 761889.

DRIVING LICENCE There is no age limit for driving a car, but after the age of 70 licences must be renewed every three years. If you have or develop a disability or medical condition that affects your ability to drive, you must by law inform the Driver Vehicle Licensing Centre (DVLC) in Swansea. Very occasionally you will be asked to take a further driving test, free of charge.

MOTABILITY If you get the mobility component of the Disability Living Allowance (DLA – see pp 26–27), you can hire a car through Motability or buy one on HP, either new or second-hand. Disabled Car Purchase is a private company that runs a similar scheme, but you do not have to receive the mobility component of DLA to qualify.

FACTFILE

► In 1994–95, 10 per cent of pensioners living alone and dependent mainly on State benefits had a car, compared to 69 per cent of the whole population.

► A 1994 survey found that 13 per cent of people aged 65 or over were unable to go out and walk down the road on their own.

For more information about Motability, contact them at Goodman House, Station Approach, Harlow, Essex CM20 2ET. Tel: 01279 635666.

For more information about the scheme run by Disabled Car Purchase, contact them at 114 Commonwealth Road, Caterham, Surrey CR3 6LS. Tel: 01883 345298.

RICA (Research Institute for Consumer Affairs) produces an *Ability Car Guide*. This consists of a folder with information on subjects such as buying a car, insurance, adaptations and breakdown services, plus factsheets on individual cars. Phone the Ability Car Team on 01992 822 820 for more details.

INSURANCE It is worth shopping round for quotes. Age Concern Insurance Services is one company that offers a good deal for older and disabled people. Some may have special restrictions, or require medical examinations each year when the contract is due for renewal, so check the wording of the policy carefully. Always shop around before taking out insurance.

VAT AND ROAD TAX People with disabilities may be exempt from road tax and from VAT on adaptations, repairs and maintenance. For further information contact RADAR.

PARKING The Orange Badge scheme allows badge-holders (either drivers or passengers) to park free at parking meters and for up to three hours on single and double yellow lines in England and Wales (there is no time limit in Scotland). Certain London boroughs run their own schemes. You may qualify if you get the higher rate of the mobility component of DLA, are registered blind, or are unable to walk or have considerable difficulty walking. Apply to your local social services department.

Access guides

Most major towns and cities publish access guides. These list local shops, theatres, restaurants and other amenities, and indicate how easy they are to use. RADAR can tell you how to get hold of these guides; it also has its own publications on access and mobility.

 For information on access guides and other publications, contact the Royal Association for Disability and Rehabilitation (RADAR), 12 City Forum, 250 City Road, London EC1V 8AF. Tel: 0171-250 3222. Textphone: 0171-250 4119.

Tripscope

Tripscope gives free information and advice on travel and transport for older and disabled people. It is not a travel agency, but it will help you plan a particular journey.

 For free information and advice about travel and transport for disabled and older people. Tel/Textphone: 0345 585641.

 For more about transport for people with disabilities, including many useful addresses and publications, see Age Concern Factsheet 26 *Travel information for older people.*

Going on holiday

For most working people holidays are limited to two or three weeks a year – for those with school-age children usually taken during the school summer holidays. Once you are retired, you have several great advantages: you have the freedom and flexibility to travel at off-peak times, you can go away more often, and you can stay away for longer. You may also have different priorities: change and stimulus may now be what you are looking for, rather than rest and relaxation.

Holiday ideas

Activity holidays

If you are looking for something a bit more stimulating than just sitting on the beach, the following are just some of the possibilities:

SPECIAL INTEREST HOLIDAYS are often advertised in specialist magazines, and sometimes in travel agents. The 'interest' can be almost anything – astrology, bridge, whist, ski-ing, gardening, antiques, painting and music to name but a few. Saga Holidays and Solo's Holidays are two of the main operators. Holt's Tours offers guided tours to First and Second World War battlefields and war graves, while Pre-Retirement Association Holiday Courses offers retirement planning holidays.

WORKING HOLIDAYS are another possibility. You could try an archaeological 'dig' or excavation. The British Trust for Conservation Volunteers also organises 'Natural Break' working holidays (see p 72).

 To find out about excavations in your area, contact the British Council for Archaeology on 01904 671417. For information about excavations abroad write to Archaeology Abroad Service, 31–34 Gordon Square, London WC1H 0PY.

TOWN TWINNING EXCHANGES with the European counterpart town are organised by many local groups. If your town has a European twin, you could ask the local council for information about related activities.

CYCLING HOLIDAYS are a wonderful way to see the countryside. Careful planning using large-scale maps is vital to ensure you see the best country, avoid the steepest hills and have somewhere to stay at night. The British Tourist Authority publishes a booklet called *Cycling* which gives details of cycling holiday operators and cycling itineraries.

WALKING HOLIDAYS are another good way to see the country. The Ramblers' Association offers walking holidays, both in this country and abroad. All holidays are carefully graded, ranging from three hours' walking a day to tough mountain walking.

ADVENTURE HOLIDAYS for the over-50s are organised by the YMCA National Centre in the Lake District, and the Youth Hostels Association has a programme of outdoor pursuits specially geared to older people who may not be used to regular exercise. Outward Bound has special holidays for the over-50s – they offer a programme of activities including abseiling, rock climbing and canoeing, an eight-day sea voyage and a highland walking holiday. Ski-ing is a perfectly viable option for older people, even first-timers, provided you are fit.

 The British Tourist Authority, Thames Tower, Blacks' Road, London W6 9EL. Tel: 0181-846 9000, can give you details of walking and cycling holidays and a great variety of adventure holidays.

Ramblers' Association, 1–5 Wandsworth Road, London SW8 2XX. Tel: 0171-582 6878.

Youth Hostels Association, YHA Groups Adviser, Westbury High Street, Napton, Rugby, Warwickshire CV23 8LZ. Tel: 01926 815169.

YMCA Centre, Lakeside, Ulverston, Cumbria LA12 8BD. Tel: 01539 531758.

For details of Outward Bound holidays phone 0990 134227.

 See Age Concern Factsheet 4 *Holidays for older people* for ideas and many useful addresses. Age Concern Books' *The World at Your Feet* (details on p 200) is full of suggestions for active and unusual holidays.

For more about study breaks and summer schools, see page 67.

Holidays for older people

Many ordinary holiday companies offer special holidays for older people. Saga is one that provides holidays exclusively for the over-50s, including many special interest holidays. It also offers a range of UK short breaks and holidays on Spain's Costa Blanca in conjunction with Age Concern. Some local Age Concern groups organise their own holidays, usually for more active older people. Such holidays are often good value, as they are able to take advantage of out-of-season and party rates.

For information about their over-50s holidays write to Saga Holidays Ltd, The Saga Building, Middelburg Square, Folkestone, Kent CT20 1BR. Freephone: 0800 300 500.

Holidays for single people

Holidays can pose particular problems for people on their own. The greatest is obviously lack of a companion, but there is also the considerable extra expense of single room supplements. However, Saga no longer has them for its UK holidays; Solo's, which specialises in group holidays for single people (age limit 69), also tries to avoid charging them.

One way round the problem of holidaying on your own is to go on an activity holiday, such as those suggested in the previous section. This ensures that you will be doing something you enjoy and meet other people with similar interests.

But this is no solution if what you enjoy is travelling round at your own pace, sightseeing and soaking up the local atmosphere. You might well find a companion through one of the friendship clubs mentioned on pages 71–72, and Travel Companions specialises in matching people to go on holiday together.

For details of their services and fees write to Travel Companions, 110 High Mount, Station Road, London NW4 3ST. Tel: 0181-202 8478.

For details of their group holidays and UK breaks, contact Solo's Holidays, 54–58 High Street, Edgware, Middlesex HA8 7ED. Tel: 0181-951 2800.

Reunion holidays

If you have relatives abroad and are thinking of a reunion visit, it might be worth joining a 'friendship club' such as CANUSPA (Canada, Australia, New Zealand and United States Parents and Associates). Lion World Travel also has four long-standing clubs. Membership entitles you to newsletters and discount flights.

If you want to combine a family visit with a sightseeing trip, both Lion World Travel and Saga will help with the arrangements.

 For more information about CANUSPA, contact Mrs Pat Roome, 72 King John Avenue, Kings Lynn, Norfolk PE30 4QZ. Tel: 01553 773097.

For details of their clubs, write to Lion World Travel Ltd, Friendship House, 49–51 Gresham Road, Staines, Middlesex TW18 2BF. Tel: 01784 465511.

Protection for travellers

For your own peace of mind, it is worth making sure the holiday firm you use is a member of the Association of British Travel Agents (ABTA). This means that their booking conditions will conform to ABTA's code of conduct, and if the firm closes down you will either get your holiday anyway or get your money back.

 If you have a complaint about a member firm, contact ABTA, 55–57 Newman Street, London W1P 4AH. Tel: 0171-637 2444.

Can you afford a holiday?

All these suggestions for holidays may well leave you rather cold if you simply can't afford one.

HOMESITTING – looking after someone else's home while they are away – can give you a free holiday, or at least a change of scene. Homesitters Ltd vet prospective homesitters, and insist that you are available for at least eight weeks a year. You get travel expenses, food and a fee.

HOME-SWAPPING, discussed on page 103, is another way of having a relatively cheap holiday.

A WORKING HOLIDAY would be another cheap option (see p 98).

 For further information about homesitting, contact Homesitters Ltd, Buckland Wharf, Buckland, Aylesbury, Bucks HP22 5LQ. Tel: 01296 630730.

Though it is not possible to get financial help for holidays from social security, some social services departments make occasional grants towards holidays. The Holiday Care Service has details of national charities which have been known to give such grants. Your local Age Concern group, town hall or CAB might know about local charities that could help.

 For information about all types of holiday for people with special needs, contact the Holiday Care Service, 2nd Floor, Imperial Buildings, Victoria Road, Horley, Surrey RH6 7PZ. Tel: 01293 774535.

Long-stay holidays

Long-stay holidays are best taken when the rest of the world is at work. April, May, September and October are good months for long-stay holidaymakers: roads, ferries and airports are less busy than at peak times, accommodation is cheaper and less booked up, yet it is warm enough for outdoor activities such as cycling, walking, camping and caravanning. Always check on local weather conditions with the national tourist office.

Long-stay packages

If your experience of holidays abroad has been mainly the annual two-week package holiday, then a long-stay package may be the best option for your first long-stay holiday. It may also be a good first step if you are considering moving abroad on a more permanent basis, as discussed on pages 130–132.

Some package holidays offer a substantial programme of daytime activities and excursions and evening entertainments. People who opt for a self-catering apartment rather than hotel accommodation are unlikely to have the same range of entertainments provided.

If you take your car with you, you could rent a cottage or farmhouse in a village or right out in the country. Many companies such as Gîtes de France offer complete packages including rented accommodation and travel.

Arranging your own holiday

The joy of arranging your own holiday is that you can plan it entirely to suit yourself. For example, you may want to stay in the old part of an interesting and well-placed town or city, but if you look through the holiday brochures, you will find that most rented properties are on the coast or in rural areas.

Finding your own accommodation to rent is best done on the spot, in advance of your stay. One good way to do this is to go on a short package holiday to the area you are thinking of staying in. If you are a car driver, you could explore an area on the way to another destination. A good place to start is the local tourist information office, which should be able to give you a list of rented properties in the area.

Home-swapping

If you like the idea of a long-stay holiday but can't really afford it, home-swapping might be a solution: you live in someone else's home for an agreed period of time, while they live in yours. Intervac and Homeline International are two agencies that arrange home swaps.

 If you are interested in home-swapping, contact Intervac, 6 Siddlas Lane, Allestree, Derby DE3 2DY. Tel: 01225 892208, or Homelink International, Linfield House, Gorse Hill Road, Virginia Water, Surrey GU25 4AS. Tel: 01344 842642.

When you have fixed up a swap, it is vital to make certain practical arrangements:

▶ Sort out who pays gas, electricity and phone bills, and the position with food in the freezer.

▶ Check with your insurance company the position regarding house contents while visitors are living in the house.

▶ Leave simple instructions for domestic appliances, basic information about local bus and train services, and emergency phone numbers for a doctor, plumber and electrician.

▶ Arrange for a neighbour to drop in and make sure all is well and to be 'on call' in case of problems.

You can save further money by agreeing to exchange cars as well, subject to satisfactory insurance arrangements.

Voluntary work abroad

Another cheap way of having a long-stay holiday is to do some work abroad as a volunteer.

The British Executive Service Overseas (BESO) needs people with management, professional or technical skills for short assignments of two or three months' duration. BESO pays the cost of air travel and insurance, while accommodation and subsistence are usually provided by the organisation requesting assistance. Voluntary Services Overseas (VSO) takes volunteers up to the age of 70.

 If you are interested in voluntary work abroad, contact BESO, 164 Vauxhall Bridge Road, London SW1V 2RB. Tel: 0171-630 0644, or VSO, 317 Putney Bridge Road, London SW15 2PN. Tel: 0181-780 2266.

 Volunteer Work, published by the Central Bureau (6th edn 1995), gives details of organisations overseas that require volunteers.

Camping and caravanning

Camping and caravanning offer great flexibility and freedom of movement, and work out a lot more cheaply than holidays that involve hotel accommodation or house rental – once you have invested in the basic equipment.

If you have never tried this kind of holiday before, it is a good idea to try out a short package holiday first with a company such as Eurocamp or Canvas Holidays. They have fully equipped luxury tents and mobile homes in sites all over Europe. Many companies offer three weeks for the price of two out of season.

If your trial run is a success, you might consider joining the Camping and Caravanning Club (CCC). Its monthly magazine has many helpful articles plus advertisements for new and second-hand caravans and equipment.

A motorised caravan is one good option for older people, as it does away with the whole business of towing, hitching and unhitching. You could try hiring caravan and equipment to begin with.

 For details of what they offer, write to the CCC, Green Fields House, Westwood Way, Coventry CV4 8JH. Tel: 01203 694995.

Things to do before going abroad

Passport and visas

If your passport needs renewing, make sure you allow plenty of time for delays at the Passport Office.

Check with the tour operator or embassy whether you will need a visa. Visas may be needed for stays over a certain length, for example 60 days in Portugal and 90 days in Spain.

Money

You will obviously need some foreign currency in cash, but it is always unwise to carry too much. For your longer-term requirements you have several choices about how you obtain money:

TRAVELLER'S CHEQUES are very safe as you have to sign them in the presence of a cashier both when you buy them and when you cash them.

EUROCHEQUES draw directly on your bank account when you need money, unlike traveller's cheques which have to be bought in advance. Make sure you keep cheques and card separate. There have been problems in using them in one or two countries, so check with your bank before you go.

CREDIT CARDS are becoming increasingly useful in Europe. Organisations such as Card Protection Plan and Credit Card Sentinel insure you against fraudulent use and provide emergency cash if your cards are stolen.

Health

IMMUNISATION Check with the appropriate embassy or your own doctor whether you need any vaccinations (your GP is entitled to charge you for this service). Alternatively you could go to a British Airways Travel Clinic, where you pay for individual advice and any necessary treatment (you do not have to be travelling with British Airways). Another source of advice is the Medical Advisory Service for Travellers Abroad (MASTA). Both BA Travel Clinics and MASTA supply items such as needle and syringe packs, mosquito nets, water purifiers and insect repellants.

EMERGENCY MEDICAL TREATMENT ABROAD In European Union countries you are entitled to treatment on a similar basis to the national population (not necessarily free). To ensure that you receive this, you must apply for form E111 before you go away. You can get this, free of charge, from a post office, on production of your passport. DSS leaflet T5 *Health Advice for Travellers* will tell you whether reciprocal arrangements exist in non-EU countries.

For the address of your nearest BA Travel Clinic, phone 0171-434 4700.

MASTA application forms are available from Boots, or phone 0171-631 4408.

Travel insurance

Travel insurance is generally sold as a 'package' and should give you all the cover you need when abroad apart from car insurance.

MEDICAL COVER You should have sufficient private medical cover to pay for comprehensive treatment in the event of illness or accident, and in case you need to be flown home. Check the policy wording carefully: many policies exclude cover for a pre-existing medical condition. To avoid possible disputes later, you should always disclose any such condition, even if you are not asked. If you already have private medical insurance, it is worth checking whether the policy gives you any cover for travel.

PERSONAL BELONGINGS AND MONEY On a long-stay holiday you may well be taking expensive items you would not normally take on holiday – a radio-cassette player, for example. Your home contents policy may contain a worldwide 'all risks' clause, but it is important to check that cover is adequate.

CANCELLATION should also be covered, as should delayed baggage, delayed departure and personal liability.

Your car

If you are taking your car abroad you will need to take with you:

▶ a full UK driving licence – check with the embassy whether you will need an international driving permit;

▶ a green card from your insurers, which is proof that you are insured against all damage you may cause to others if you are involved in an accident;

▶ a bail bond if you are travelling in Spain.

It is also advisable to take your car registration document.

Up-to-date, detailed advice on taking your car abroad is available from the AA or RAC.

 For more about arranging to go abroad, see Age Concern Books' *The World at Your Feet* (details on p 200).

Home security

Ideally, you want to give the impression that your house is still occupied – an obviously empty house is an invitation to burglars. The well-known give-away clues that indicate an absent owner are uncut grass and free newspapers or junk mail stuck in a letterbox or lying in the porch. There is no substitute for getting someone to keep an eye on the place for you, removing these eyesores and if possible switching lights on and off, drawing curtains and so on. You might even consider paying someone a nominal caretaking allowance.

If you defrost the fridge or freezer, don't leave the door wide open – a clear indication to a burglar that the house is unoccupied. Instead, stick a wedge of paper in to stop the door closing.

Finally, always tell the insurance company that covers your property and contents if you are going to be away for more than a couple of weeks. They may insist on extra security precautions if cover is to be maintained.

If you are planning a long stay

If you are planning a long-stay holiday, there are some other things you will need to consider:

PAYING BILLS You could set up a monthly direct debit or standing order from your bank or building society account to pay gas, electricity, phone and other bills likely to arrive in your absence. If your credit card is directly linked to your bank, you could arrange to pay your credit card bill out of funds in your current account.

STATE RETIREMENT PENSION OR WIDOW'S BENEFIT If you receive your pension by weekly order book and are going abroad for less than three months, you can cash all the orders when you come home. If you are going away for more than three months, you will have to contact your local Benefits Agency (social security) office and arrange to have your pension paid into a bank or building society account. If you already have your pension paid this way, you do not have to inform the Benefits Agency unless you are going to be away for more than six months. Alternatively, you can arrange to have your pension paid to you abroad.

OTHER STATE BENEFITS You should contact your Benefits Agency (social security) office or local authority to find out whether your benefit is affected by your absence.

ROAD TAX AND CAR INSURANCE If you are leaving your car at home, you might look into getting a refund on your insurance. For a refund of road tax your car will need to be off the public highway.

Holidays for people with disabilities

If you are disabled, arranging a holiday can seem almost impossibly daunting, but there are a number of organisations that may help:

HOLIDAY CARE SERVICE is a charity that gives free information and advice on holidays for people with disabilities. It also has a factsheet listing organisations that provide escorts for people who cannot – or do not want to – travel alone.

LOCAL AGE CONCERN GROUPS sometimes organise holidays specially for frail or disabled people. If not, they may know of other agencies in the area that do.

LOCAL AUTHORITY SOCIAL SERVICES DEPARTMENTS sometimes have their own accommodation for elderly and disabled people.

RADAR (Royal Association for Disability and Rehabilitation) publishes holiday factsheets and books, including *Holidays in the British Isles* and *Holidays and Travel Abroad*, updated annually, which covers 110 countries.

CHARITIES such as Arthritis Care and the Multiple Sclerosis Society often provide information on holidays, and some have their own holiday homes or organise holidays for special groups.

For specialist advice on holidays for people with disabilities and respite care, contact the Holiday Care Service, 2nd Floor, Imperial Buildings, Victoria Road, Horley, Surrey RH6 7PZ. Tel: 01293 774535.

For a list of their holiday factsheets and books, or information about respite care, contact RADAR, 12 City Forum, 250 City Road, London EC1V 8AF. Tel: 0171-250 3222.

 For more about holidays for older and disabled people, and for carers, including the addresses of many useful organisations, see Age Concern Factsheet 4 *Holidays for older people.*

Holidays for carers

If you are a carer and want a holiday break, it may be possible for a bed to be found in a hospital or local authority residential home for the person you care for. Ask your GP or the local social services department.

If the person you care for wants to stay at home while you are away, the Holiday Care Service can provide information about agencies that can arrange for care in the home.

Financial help may be available through social security towards the cost of short-term care for those on very low incomes.

 For a free booklet about respite care called *Taking a Break*, send an sae to the King's Fund, 11–13 Cavendish Square, London W1M 0AN. Tel: 0171-307 2400.

Your home

Does your present home suit you? Is it likely to go on suiting you as you grow older? As far as your housing situation is concerned, now is the time

> ▶ **To move or not to move?**
> ▶ **Repairs and improvements**
> ▶ **Moving abroad**

to think ahead. Moving house is always a great upheaval, but one that you will probably be better able to cope with now than later.

If you want to stay living where you are, now could be the best time to get repairs and improvements done, when you are as physically fit and as financially well off as you are ever likely to be.

For those who have always yearned for a complete change, this could be the time to try living abroad.

To move or not to move?

The first decision to be made is whether or not to move from your present home. If you don't think it is likely to continue to suit you as you grow older, you may well decide to move now. Most retired people move into another ordinary house, but some may like the idea of moving into housing specially designed for older people. This section looks at the various housing options, including those open to tenants and people with limited capital, who have fewer choices than those with more capital.

Points to consider

If you are considering whether you should move house, here are some questions you might ask yourself:

▶ Do you like the area, and is it likely to change in the near future?

▶ Are you near relatives and friends?

▶ Are you near shops, public transport and other amenities?

▶ Is your home expensive to run – in particular, to heat?

▶ Is it easy to clean and maintain?

▶ Is it larger than you need?

▶ Is it in need of repair or likely to need major repairs in the next few years?

If you do decide to move, you will obviously need to look at your proposed new home just as critically as you looked at your old one. And if you are thinking of moving to a new area, the following points might also be worth considering:

▶ If you are moving to be nearer relatives, you may not know many other people in the new area and may end up missing the friends you now have. The relatives you are moving nearer to could themselves move away from the area in the future.

▶ If you are a couple and one of you dies, will the other still want to live in that area?

▶ Is the area noisy in the daytime, as you are likely to be at home much more than previously?

▶ Is the area as convenient as where you live at present in terms of shops, transport, doctor, library, pub, etc?

▶ Is the outside of the house and the surrounding area well lit at night? Would you feel secure there?

It might also be worth looking much further ahead: for example, would it be possible to put in a bathroom downstairs if someone in the family began to find the stairs difficult? A house with very steep stairs might not be a good choice.

Moving to retirement housing

Specially designed housing without a scheme manager

Many local authorities and housing associations have housing for rent which is either purpose-built or converted specially for older people, but without the support of a warden or scheme manager, and many private companies sell similar housing.

Such schemes are usually within easy reach of shops, public transport and other services, and in a relatively flat area. Special design features might include level or ramped access, wide doorways, waist-high sockets and switches, and walk-in showers.

If you are thinking of buying a home that is said to be specially suitable for older people, you should make sure that it does have most of these features. Some housing that is marketed as being designed for older people is in fact barely different from ordinary housing.

Retirement housing with a scheme manager

Retirement housing for rent is provided mainly by local councils and housing associations. In recent years demand for this type of housing has been very heavy, so it is now quite difficult to find. You can also buy retirement housing, both from private companies and from housing associations.

 For more information on rented retirement housing, see Age Concern booklet *Getting and Paying for Rented Sheltered Housing* or Factsheet 8 *Rented accommodation for older people.*

Retirement housing schemes usually consist of between 20 and 40 self-contained one- or two-bedroomed flats, bungalows or houses, with a resident scheme manager and a 24-hour alarm in each home for emergency use. Both tenants and owner-occupiers pay a service charge for the cost of the scheme manager and other services.

Retirement housing schemes normally have a guest room and laundry facilities, and many also have a common room or lounge for use by all residents. The extent to which residents socialise with each other varies from scheme to scheme.

The role of the scheme manager also varies. Retirement housing is generally intended for fairly independent people, so the scheme manager will not normally help with shopping, cooking, cleaning or personal tasks such as dressing, bathing or nursing. Most will keep a discreet eye on residents, and call for help in an emergency. They may call on

FACTFILE

► In 1994 64 per cent of households containing people aged 65 or over lived in owner-occupied accommodation compared with 68 per cent of the rest of the population.

► Seven out of ten people who own their home outright are aged 60 or over.

► Only 55 per cent of people aged 80 or over are homeowners.

residents each day to check all is well. If residents need services such as meals on wheels or home help, the scheme manager may be able to arrange this.

Some 'very sheltered' or 'extra care' schemes may include facilities and services for some people who cannot live totally independently. These may be provided in the resident's own home or in a special part of the scheme. Even if you do not envisage needing such facilities for many years, moving into a scheme of this type might enable you to stay in your retirement home – or scheme – for longer than you would otherwise have been able to do.

 Types of housing that provide a greater degree of support are discussed further on page 180. For information about almshouses, see pages 119–120.

Buying retirement housing

Many developers (and some local councils and housing associations) sell sheltered housing for older people. Once all the properties in a scheme have been sold, the developer usually hands the scheme to a separate management organisation (often a housing association), which assumes responsibility for running it. Schemes are normally leasehold, with services such as cleaning and maintenance of common areas.

When buying a new property, you are strongly recommended to buy it only from a builder registered with the National House Building Council (NHBC). The NHBC has a code of practice applying to all retirement housing sold after 1 April 1990.

 A list of developers selling retirement housing for older people is available from Sheltered Housing Services Ltd, 8–9 Abbey Parade, London W5 1EE. Tel: 0181-997 9313.

Lists of retirement housing schemes for sale and rent are also available from the Elderly Accommodation Council, 46A Chiswick High Road, London W4 1SZ. Tel: 0181-742 1182/995 8320.

If you are thinking of buying retirement housing, you should consider the following points:

► Is the area relatively flat, and is the scheme conveniently placed for public transport, shops and other services?

► Does the design of the flat include most of the features mentioned on page 113?

► What facilities are there for residents' use?

► Would you be able to fit your furniture in the flat?

► How experienced are the builder and management organisation at providing retirement housing? Do they belong to the Association of Retirement Housing Managers, whose members have to follow a code of practice?

► How much is the service charge and what does it cover? What else will you have to pay for, for example ground rent?

► If, as should be the case, there is a separate 'sinking' fund for repairs, how do residents contribute to it?

► What are the arrangements if you want to resell? Do you get back the full market value?

► What are the scheme manager's main duties, and what are the arrangements when he or she is off duty?

► Does the lease cover what happens if your health deteriorates?

As soon as you have paid a reservation fee to the developer, you should be given a Purchaser's Information Pack (PIP) covering all these points.

 For more about buying retirement housing, see Age Concern Factsheet 2 *Retirement housing for sale* or Age Concern Books' *A Buyer's Guide to Retirement Housing* (details on p 203).

Options for people with limited capital

If you live in a flat or in housing which is not in very good condition, you may find that after selling up you cannot afford to buy another home outright. This may also apply if you want to move to a more expensive area.

If you are in this position, your options may be rather limited, but special schemes do exist which may provide a solution.

Shared ownership

A few councils and housing associations run 'shared ownership' schemes, under which you can part-buy and part-rent a property. The maximum share you can own is usually around 75 per cent; you will normally have to pay rent on the remainder as well as a service charge. If you leave the scheme you receive your share of the property's value at the time of your leaving.

Most shared ownership schemes are not designed specifically for older people, but a few housing associations do offer retirement housing on a shared ownership basis.

Interest-only mortgages

You may have difficulty getting an ordinary mortgage to top up your capital, but you may be able to get an interest-only mortgage from a building society (see p 45). You pay the interest, but the capital is not repaid until you die or the property is eventually sold.

Schemes for buying retirement housing

The following schemes apply mainly to retirement housing or other housing specially designed for older people:

LEASEHOLD SCHEMES FOR THE ELDERLY (LSE) allow you to buy at 70 per cent of the purchase price and receive back 70 per cent of the property's value when you sell. No new LSE schemes are being built, but some LSE properties may be available as resales.

LOAN-STOCK SCHEMES are run by a very few housing associations and charities: you can 'buy' by making an interest-free loan to the trust or charity. When you leave, you normally get back the sum you paid, without interest and with some deductions (eg for administering the resale). You should check carefully exactly what your rights as a resident will be.

BUYING AT A DISCOUNT means you get back only a percentage of the value of the property when you resell it: if you buy at 80 per cent of the full price you will get back only 80 per cent of its value. Be wary of developers offering to give you back less of a share in the property than you originally bought.

BUYING A LIFE-SHARE IN SHELTERED HOUSING is a scheme by which you buy the right to live in a property for life at a percentage of the purchase price; when you die the whole value of the property passes to the finance company. Few, if any, developers offer such schemes, but if you are considering one you should take legal and professional advice.

Moving to rented accommodation

If you want to move house and cannot afford to buy what you want, you may consider moving into rented accommodation.

The main sources of rented accommodation are local councils and housing associations. Moving into private rented accommodation is less likely to be a good choice for most older people, largely because of anxieties about rent levels and security of tenure. Always get advice before signing a tenancy agreement with a private landlord, or you may find yourself left with few rights.

Your local council, housing advice centre, CAB or local Age Concern group should be able to give you information about rented housing in your area.

For more information on renting from local councils and housing associations, see Age Concern Factsheet 8 *Rented accommodation for older people*.

For more information on private tenancies, see Age Concern Factsheet 36 *Private tenants' rights*.

Age Concern England has a list of housing associations which offer accommodation for older people for each county in England and for each London borough. Send a 9″ × 12″ sae to the Information and Policy Department, 1268 London Road, London SW16 4ER, stating which county or borough you are interested in.

Many councils and housing associations will not consider homeowners for rehousing in rented accommodation, so homeowners who cannot get enough for their homes to enable them to buy another property can find themselves in an unfortunate trap.

APPLYING FOR COUNCIL OR HOUSING ASSOCIATION HOUSING Your first step is to put yourself on the waiting list: unfortunately many councils and housing associations have very long waiting lists. If you wish to apply for housing in a different area, you may find that the council or housing association will not consider applicants from outside the area. The HOMES Mobility Scheme exists to enable people to move to be near relatives or for other strong social reasons, but you normally need to be a council or housing association tenant already or high on the waiting list.

HOUSING ASSOCIATION TENANCIES If you become a housing association tenant, you will usually be given an 'assured tenancy', unlike people who became tenants before 1 January 1989, who will be 'secure' tenants. This means you will not have the right to have your rent registered with the local Rent Officer, who sets rents for people with secure tenancies, so you may find the rent high in some areas.

Assured tenants nevertheless have considerable rights, and cannot normally be asked to leave unless they fail to keep to their tenancy conditions.

 For more information about council and housing association tenants' rights see Age Concern Factsheet 35 *Rights for council and housing association tenants.*

ALMSHOUSES Most almshouses date back many centuries, having been provided by landowners and other benefactors for older people in need. Most have been fully modernised, and there are also newly built flats and bungalows. Some are warden-assisted.

Almshouses are provided rent-free, but there may be a weekly mainte-nance contribution. Many consider only local applicants but exceptions can be made if the applicant has a connection with the area.

Residents of almshouses are considered to be licensees rather than ten-ants, so their rights are not as secure as other housing association ten-ants. If you or an older relative are thinking of moving into an almshouse, it would be wise to get advice from a solicitor, CAB or hous-ing advice centre first.

Information on almshouses can be obtained from the Almshouse Association, Billingbear Lodge, Carters Hill, Wokingham, Berkshire RG40 5RU. Tel: 01344 52922.

Options for existing tenants

Exchanges

If you are already a council or housing association tenant and you want to move within your area, you can ask for a transfer, but this could take years. Most councils and housing associations allow tenants to exchange with each other, but this obviously depends on someone else wanting to live in your home.

If you want to move to another area, the council or housing association may have 'reciprocal' arrangements to rehouse a certain number of applicants from another area. A very small number of people achieve a move through the HOMES Mobility Scheme; contact your local council or housing association for details.

By contrast, any council or housing association tenant can attempt to swap homes with another on their own initiative through the Homeswap scheme, but this is not usually a realistic option for tenants living in poor housing.

A leaflet called *Homeswaps* should be available from your council housing department, housing advice centre or CAB.

Tenants' right to buy

COUNCIL TENANTS If you have been a council tenant for at least two years, you will usually have the right to buy your home from the council. You will be entitled to a discount on the market price based on how long you have lived in your home. If you sell within three years of buying, you may have to repay some of the discount.

HOUSING ASSOCIATION TENANTS Most secure tenants of non-charitable housing associations also have the right to buy. Assured tenants generally do not have the right to buy, although some associations choose to offer tenants this right.

TENANTS' INCENTIVE SCHEME If you are a housing association tenant, you may also be able to get a grant under the Tenants' Incentive Scheme to enable you to move out of your home and buy another property privately. Ask your housing association for details.

If you live in sheltered housing or any other housing which is particularly suitable for older people, you will have the right to buy only if the property was first let after 1 January 1990.

If you are thinking of exercising your right to buy, you may be able to get an interest-only mortgage, usually from a building society but sometimes from the council (see p 45). If you have been getting Housing Benefit to help with your rent, you may be able to get some help from Income Support towards the mortgage repayments.

If you cannot afford the full price or cannot get a big enough mortgage, you could enquire about buying your home on a shared ownership basis (see p 45).

> **FACTFILE**
>
> ▶ 36 per cent of people aged 65 or over rent their homes.
>
> ▶ 30 per cent live in either council or housing association accommodation.

Before going ahead it is worth checking if there are plans for major repairs or improvements to your block in the future, as you would be liable for your share of the cost.

For more information about tenants' right to buy, see the Government leaflet *Your Right to Buy Your Home*, available from councils, housing advice centres and CABs, or ring the Department of the Environment Publications Line on 0181-691 9191.

For more information about the various housing options, see Age Concern Books' *Housing Options for Older People* (details on p 203).

Buying a freehold

If you live in a leasehold flat, you may have the right to join with other leaseholders and collectively buy the freehold, under legislation introduced in the Housing and Urban Development Act 1993.

This would be particularly advantageous for anyone who has a short lease, which is otherwise a diminishing asset. In addition, some leaseholders are not happy with the management service they receive from the freeholder.

Repairs and improvements

Around the time of your retirement is a good time to make a thorough assessment of what condition your home is in. If repair work or maintenance is needed, or is likely to be needed in the next few years, or if there are improvements to your home that you would like to make, it might be wise to get the work done now, when you may be able to do some of it yourself. You could use some of the lump sum from an occupational or personal pension for this purpose.

Deciding what needs to be done

If there is a housing improvement service in your area – often called 'Care and Repair' or 'Staying Put' – they will give specialist advice to older homeowners. They will normally offer practical help with such tasks as arranging a survey, getting estimates from reliable builders, applying for grants or building society loans, and keeping an eye on the work as it progresses. Agency services are non-profit-making, but they may charge a fee towards staff and other costs. This can normally be included in the grant or loan, if you are receiving one.

> To find out if there is a housing improvement agency in your area, contact your local Age Concern group, your local council's improvement grants section or the national office of Care and Repair (England), Castle House, Kirtley Drive, Nottingham NG7 1LD. Tel: 0115 979 9091.

If there is no housing improvement agency in your area, it may well be worth considering having a professional survey done by an architect or surveyor, especially if you live in an older property. Before any surveyor inspects your property you should ask what the fee will be – you will have to pay this even if no repair work is carried out.

Contact your local CAB or the Royal Institution of Chartered Surveyors, 12 Great George Street, London SW1P 3AD. Tel: 0171-222 7000, for details of the Chartered Surveyors Voluntary Service, which aims to help people who would otherwise be unable to get professional advice. You will need to be referred to them by a CAB or other local advice agency.

The Royal Institute of British Architects, 66 Portland Place, London W1N 4AD. Tel: 0171-580 5533, can help you find an architect.

If you are going to check things over yourself, you should look at the following areas:

ROOF Inspect both outside (using binoculars) and inside (via the loft). Look out for broken or missing tiles, and inspect the supporting timbers for damp or white patches or any sign of woodworm or rot (the timber affected will be soft and spongy).

CHIMNEYS AND EXTERNAL WALLS Look for signs of crumbling brickwork and cracking or damaged mortar. Rendered walls need to be repainted regularly (unless they have never been painted) and any loose rendering needs to be replaced. Make sure that air bricks are undamaged and clear of fallen leaves and soil.

DOORS AND WINDOWS All external paintwork needs regular repainting, and draught strip material may need replacing. Check window frames for damaged putty and rotten wood.

GUTTERING Cast-iron pipes should be repainted regularly – or replaced with plastic ones. Make sure gutters are securely fixed and not blocked with leaves or dirt.

PLUMBING Check all joints in pipes and fixtures to make sure there are no leaks – white or green marks are a warning sign.

WIRING If your wiring is over 15 years old, have it checked by a professional electrician. If you get your house rewired, you might want to place new sockets at waist height. You might also want to consider some lighting to the outside of your house, as this is a great deterrent to intruders.

FLOORS Check for signs of woodworm or dry rot.

Specialist firms will give you a free survey of floor and roof timbers. They will then guarantee any work carried out.

You can reduce your maintenance costs significantly by using good quality paint and building materials and by fitting items such as aluminium window frames and doors that need almost no maintenance.

Finding a builder

If there is no housing agency service in your area, there is no easy way to find a good builder. Friends' recommendations may be fine for small jobs, but for larger ones you should always employ a builder backed by a proper guarantee scheme. With the Federation of Master Builders (FMB) scheme, the National Register of Warranted Builders, you pay a premium equivalent to 1 per cent of the cost of the work, but it will probably be money well spent. You should always get two or three estimates from different builders before making your final choice.

 Information on the FMB scheme and a list of builders registered under it can be obtained from the FMB, Gordon Fisher House, 14–15 Great James Street, London WC1N 3DP. Tel: 0171-242 7583.

Financial help with repairs and improvements

You may be able to get a home improvement grant from your local council to help with the cost of repairs. There are three types of grant:

RENOVATION GRANTS help towards the cost of major repairs and improvements to your home, such as installing an inside toilet or a hot and cold water supply. All grants are discretionary; they will depend on your income and savings and the council's priorities.

HOME REPAIRS ASSISTANCE can help towards the cost of smaller repairs, improvements and adaptations, including improving energy efficiency and home security. The maximum grant is £2,000. Help is available to anyone over 60 or 'disabled and infirm'; councils have considerable discretion in deciding who should get assistance.

DISABLED FACILITIES GRANTS See pages 172–173.

If you are on Income Support, you may be able to get a grant or loan from the Social Fund (see p 23). If you cannot get a grant and need to carry out essential repairs or improvements, you might be able to get an interest-only loan against the value of your home. You pay the interest, but the capital is not repaid until the property is eventually sold. If you are on Income Support, you may receive some extra benefit to cover interest payments. The fact that no tax relief is available on loans for home improvements or repairs can make the repayments high for people who do not receive help through Income Support.

 For more information on financial help with repairs, see Age Concern Factsheet 13 *Older homeowners: financial help with repairs and adaptations.* If there is a home improvement agency in your area, they should be able to give you advice on sources of financial help.

Insulation and draughtproofing

As you get older, you are likely to feel the cold more. Both for your own comfort and to save on heating bills, it is worth considering what you can do to reduce heat loss from your home.

DRAUGHTPROOFING As much as a quarter of all heat lost from homes is through draughts from floors, doors and windows. Draughtproofing doors and windows (but not in kitchens and bathrooms), and sealing gaps between skirtings and floor and around pipes and cables, will all help.

LOFT INSULATION A further quarter of all heat lost is through the roof. You should have insulation material at least 100 mm (4 in) and preferably 150 mm (6 in) thick between the ceiling joists. This usually comes in the form of a glass-fibre quilt. If you do fit this yourself you should always wear a dust mask and gloves. Make sure you:

► insulate hot and cold water pipes and tanks, but not underneath the cold water tank, since warmth from below will help stop it freezing;

► insulate and draughtproof the loft hatch;

► leave sufficient air-gaps between the eaves to avoid condensation, which can rot timbers.

WALL INSULATION The greatest single area of heat loss in most homes is through the walls – up to 35 per cent. If your house has unfilled cavity walls, having them insulated will cut down your heating bills enormously and should pay for itself within five years or so. You will need a contractor to do this. If cavity wall insulation is not possible, you could consider insulating the walls on the inside or outside, but this is much more expensive. Lining the walls behind radiators with foil or aluminium sheets can help reduce heat loss, particularly on external walls.

WINDOWS In addition to draughtproofing, you can reduce heat loss through windows by using heavy, lined curtains (behind not in front of radiators) and fitting shelves above radiators under windows – about 75 mm (3 in) above is ideal. Double glazing is a good idea if you are replacing windows anyway. Otherwise you can fit secondary glazing – a single pane of glass – to your windows. Plastic glazing material clipped on to your windows – or even thin plastic film taped on – is cheaper, but it needs to be replaced regularly and looks unattractive.

DOORS Apart from draughtproofing, you can reduce heat loss by fixing a cover to the inside of your letter box, hanging a curtain over the door, and attaching draught strips (brushes) to the bottom of the door – or you can use a traditional sausage dog.

HOT WATER CYLINDER JACKET Fitting a hot water cylinder jacket can pay for itself almost in a matter of weeks provided it is thick enough (at least 75 mm – 3 in).

Financial help with insulation and draughtproofing

Anyone over pension age may be able to get a grant under the Home Energy Efficiency Scheme towards the cost of insulation of lofts, pipes, and hot and cold water tanks; cavity wall insulation; heating system controls; draughtproofing; and basic energy advice. If you cannot do the work yourself, you can ask a local 'network installer' to do it.

Only people receiving certain State benefits will be able to receive the maximum grant (£305 in 1997–98). Others will have to contribute 75 per cent of the cost.

To find out more about installers in your area, and to get more information on how to apply for a grant, contact the Energy Action Grants Agency, Freepost, PO Box 1NG, Eldon Square, Newcastle Upon Tyne NE99 2RP. Freephone: 0800 181 667.

For advice, contact Neighbourhood Energy Action, St Andrew's House, 90–92 Pilgrim Street, Newcastle Upon Tyne NE1 6SG. Tel: 0191-261 5677.

You may be able to get home repairs assistance from your local council to help with the cost of draughtproofing and insulation (see p 125).

Heating and ventilation

Heating

Having ensured that your home is well insulated, it is sensible to consider whether your heating system is energy-efficient and economical to run. If you do not have central heating, you could consider installing it. If your central heating boiler is more than ten years old, it may be worth replacing it: one of the new high-energy ones could reduce your fuel bills by as much as 25–30 per cent.

FACTFILE

▶ In 1994–95, fewer than 74 per cent of pensioners mainly dependent on State benefits and living alone had central heating compared to over 84 per cent of all households.

▶ In 1995 (England and Wales) 265 people over pension age had hypothermia given as the underlying cause of death on their death certificates.

An older central heating system may have rather basic controls. More sophisticated controls – which allow you, for example, to set different temperatures at different times of day – could save you money. Fitting thermostats or time clocks to individual heaters could also help.

Sources of help and advice

▶ Both gas and electricity companies offer advice on the best way to use appliances and how to make your heating system more effective. Telephone the customer services number on your fuel bill to arrange for an adviser to visit.

▶ British Gas runs a Gas Care Register: if you are over 60, you may qualify for a free annual safety check on gas appliances. If your appliance is dangerous, the engineer has to disconnect it.

 For information on heating between October and March, contact the **Winter Warmthline** on Freephone 0800 289 404; Textphone 0800 269 626. This is run by Age Concern, Help the Aged and Neighbourhood Energy Action.

Ventilation

Open fires, gas fires, flued boilers and flueless appliances such as paraffin or bottled gas heaters and gas cookers all need a good supply of fresh air to burn safely and efficiently. You can ensure there is a good supply of air into the room by fitting an air brick or trickle ventilator.

Lack of ventilation can also lead to condensation. The poorer the ventilation and the colder the house, the greater the risk. As much moisture as possible should be removed by:

▶ opening windows while cooking or drying clothes;

▶ fitting trickle ventilators or an extractor fan;

▶ not draughtproofing kitchen or bathroom windows (but you can draughtproof the internal doors to keep moisture from spreading through the house).

 For more information on all aspects of repairs and maintenance, see Age Concern Books' *Your Home in Retirement* (details on p 203).

Moving abroad

Thousands of Britons dream of moving abroad to a warmer climate when they retire, and in recent years the number of people actually turning their dream into reality has risen significantly. If you are contemplating such a move, great caution is needed. You should consider all the pitfalls of moving house mentioned above – and more: if you worry about missing your friends if you move to a different area within the UK, how much more isolated you could feel in another country.

Keeping your options open

There is a lot to be said for keeping your options open. You may well enjoy living abroad in the early years of your retirement but find you wish to return to the UK as you get older and less active.

Keeping a UK base

Keeping your property in the UK will make it much easier for you to move back. If you sell your house, you may find yourself unable to afford a similar property on your return if house prices rise disproportionately in the UK.

If you do decide to retain a UK base, you may consider letting your home while you are away. It is never a good idea for properties to stay empty for a long time, and the 1988 and 1996 Housing Acts make it possible for owner-occupiers to let their property in the confidence of getting it back when they want it.

Renting rather than buying

Another way of keeping your options open is to rent rather than buy a home abroad. Renting gives you the chance to make sure you like living abroad – and the location you have chosen – before you actually commit yourself to buying anything.

If you do decide to rent, at least at first, you could try local estate agents (although there are not as many as in the UK), advertisements in local newspapers or, in a tourist area, the local tourist office, as you would for a long-stay holiday (see p 103).

Buying property abroad

The most essential rule for anyone buying property abroad is to take independent professional advice. Be wary of developers who say their lawyers have checked everything: you need a lawyer who is acting for you, who puts your interests first. There are UK firms of solicitors who specialise in the purchase of foreign property.

 For a list of addresses of legal firms who specialise in foreign purchase, contact the Law Society, 113 Chancery Lane, London WC2A 1SX. Tel: 0171-242 1222.

As far as finding a property is concerned, there are specialist magazines such as *International Property Magazine*, available from most news-agents. This includes homes for sale or rent plus holiday lettings. Property developers are often represented at retirement exhibitions. In addition, many of the larger UK estate agents are now opening overseas departments.

Finding the right place

The travel features in the Saturday issues of most of the quality daily papers and in the quality Sunday press may well be of interest, as they often focus on lesser-known parts of a country. Above all, look around yourself. Be prepared to make more than one trip to your chosen country, and see as many properties as possible while you are there.

Once you have chosen a place, it is always wise to try living there for at least a few months before committing yourself – both to experience the climate at different times of year and to get a general feel of what it is like to live there. The fact that you have enjoyed a holiday in a place does not mean you will enjoy living there permanently, especially if you went there some time ago – places change very rapidly. It is always worth talking to other people who have been retired there some years.

Factors to bear in mind

CAN YOU AFFORD IT? House prices abroad may seem temptingly cheap, but you will have to live too. The rate of inflation in the country of your choice and fluctuations in exchange rates are factors beyond your control. Additional expenses to be considered are the costs of medical insurance and perhaps of visits to the UK.

WHAT ABOUT YOUR PENSION? If you are under State Pension age, check with the Department of Social Security (DSS) that you have a full contribution record (see pp 13–14). If not, you may want to pay voluntary NI contributions. If you are already drawing your pension, you can arrange to have it paid to you anywhere abroad, but outside the European Union you will receive annual increases in your pension only if you are living in a country which has reciprocal arrangements with the UK.

WHAT ABOUT TAX? The rules governing whether you are resident or non-resident for UK tax purposes are extremely complex – even the timing of your departure can affect your tax bill. If you own property in another country, you may be liable to pay tax there. You will need to take professional advice about your tax position.

IS IT WORTH TAKING YOUR FURNITURE WITH YOU? A specialist removal firm will be able to advise you about what items are not worth taking. Some UK electrical appliances, for example, may be unsuitable for use abroad.

CAN YOU TAKE YOUR PETS? Always ask your vet's advice first. Pets will usually have to spend a few days in quarantine on arrival, but dogs and cats have to spend six months in quarantine on return to the UK.

WILL YOU WANT TO WORK? You may have stated in your application for permanent residence that you do not intend to work. If you are offered part-time work, you should seek professional advice before accepting.

WHAT IF YOU WANT TO RETURN AND CLAIM INCOME SUPPORT? Under the 'habitual residence' rules, people who have entered the UK within five years of making a claim, including British citizens, will be asked about this and could be refused benefit.

Staying healthy

If you retire at around 60 you may have a third of your life ahead of you. How much you get out of it will depend partly on your state of

health, so retirement seems a good time to give some thought to your body and to making sure it is in as good shape as possible for the years to come.

Looking after your body

Many people who lead busy working lives neglect their bodies over the years. They may not have time for regular exercise, they may often find themselves falling back on convenience foods, they may never have found the ideal moment to give up smoking. People often tend to feel that by the time they reach retirement the damage has already been done and it is not worth making the effort to change. But it is never too late: positive benefits can be reaped from changes in your lifestyle whatever your age.

Taking exercise

Recent research has shown that people who remain fit and active are healthier and less likely to die of heart disease and a range of other illnesses than those who take less exercise. Generally, it is the years of inactivity, rather than ageing as such, that cause the deterioration in physical fitness.

The good news is that fitness can be regained: almost everyone over the age of 50, whatever their health problems, can benefit from exercise, provided it is gentle and safe. If you start exercising regularly in retirement, you may end up fitter than you have been for years.

The following are some of the advantages of taking regular exercise as you get older:

► It will make you feel more energetic.

► It helps keep you supple and prevents stiffness in your spine and joints.

► It maintains muscle strength.

► It helps keep your weight under control.

► It helps prevent osteoporosis (which mainly affects women but does also affect men – see pp 165–167).

► It can make you feel better and look better. How you hold yourself, your complexion and your shape could all improve.

If you have always taken regular exercise, obviously all you need to do is carry on – even if you do find it gradually more difficult than you used to. Retirement could also provide an ideal opportunity for you to try some other sporting activity you have never done before.

What exercise is suitable?

People who don't like the idea of exercise will often cite the proverbial case of the 55-year-old first-time jogger who drops down dead in his tracks. If you have a health problem or haven't exercised for years, it is obviously wise to check with your GP first. And be careful to increase the length and intensity of your activity gradually. The Sports Council's advice is to stop immediately if you feel any unpleasant effects such as pain or dizziness. A good rule of thumb is that you should be able to talk to someone while you are exercising.

FACTFILE

The Allied Dunbar National Fitness Survey (1992) found:

► 40 per cent of men and women aged 65–74 do not take part in any moderate or vigorous activity.

► 30 per cent of men and 50 per cent of women aged 65–74 do not have sufficient strength in the thigh muscles to rise easily from a low chair.

► Among women aged over 55, only 50 per cent have sufficient leg power to climb stairs easily.

Activities to avoid for people who are not fit and active are those which involve too much exertion or strain. Squash, jogging and aerobics might be too strenuous for the unfit – as well as jarring to the knees and hips. Both walking and swimming are ideal all-round forms of exercise. Most sports or leisure centres offer exercise classes for the over-50s. They may also offer special taster sessions for older people. Table tennis, short-mat bowling and racketball are all sociable indoor activities that do not require too much exertion, ideal for the less fit.

Any vigorous exercise session should start with a gradual warm-up. This means that you get the circulation going and get oxygenised blood into the muscles and joints before performing more vigorous actions. It's also good to start and finish with some stretching exercises. This helps keep you supple and reduces the risk of injury. Only stretch as much as is comfortable and never bounce while doing a stretch.

 The Sports Council has a Sportsline on 0171-222 8000 which can give you information about the clubs nearest you where you can participate in the sport of your choice.

For information about sports facilities for disabled people, regional Sports Council offices all have a disability liaison officer. Ring 0171-273 1500 for the phone number of your nearest office.

Walking

Walking regularly (and briskly) provides good exercise – though it does not do much to increase suppleness. If you get bored with the same old route every day, you could try a guided walk occasionally. These take place in towns and in the country. There are usually leaflets in libraries giving dates and meeting places and a rough idea of the distance. For longer walks you could see if there is a local Ramblers' Association group.

Swimming

Swimming is an excellent all-round form of exercise: it uses many different muscles as well as stimulating the heart and circulation. It is particularly good for people with arthritis as the water supports the body and takes the weight off painful joints. It is not, however, as helpful in the prevention of osteoporosis as weight-bearing exercise such as walking.

You don't have to be able to swim already: many pools offer special classes for older non-swimmers. If you already swim well, you might like to take a life-saving certificate, or help at a swimming session for disabled people.

Cycling

Cycling is the most energy-efficient way of getting about, and it is also good exercise. It doesn't matter if you haven't done it for years: as with swimming, once you have learned to ride a bike you never forget.

Cycling in big towns in heavy traffic is both dangerous and unpleasant, but if you choose the right roads and the right time of day cycling is a good way to get about. Town planners are increasingly trying to provide cycle lanes and cycle routes, and local cycling groups such as the London Cycling Campaign publish route maps which avoid main roads.

Once you have built up confidence with local trips, you might like to arm yourself with Ordnance Survey maps and explore the surrounding countryside. If you prefer the idea of cycling in a group, the Cyclists' Touring Club will give you details of local activities. In addition to their touring information, they offer members expert technical advice, free legal aid and free third-party insurance.

 For more information about the Cyclists' Touring Club, write to them at 69 Meadrow, Godalming, Surrey GU7 3HS. Tel: 01483 417217.

Exercise classes

Most leisure and sports centres run keep-fit classes for the over-50s, as do adult education services. Extend is an educational charity which specialises in movement to music classes for older people. You can write to them to find out if they have a class near you.

Dancing also provides good exercise. There are many kinds on offer: line, jazz, modern, ballroom, country, Scottish, tap.

Another increasingly popular activity, particularly among older people, is Tai-chi. Originally a Chinese martial art, it consists of a series of slow choreographed movements and helps improve muscle strength, balance and breathing. Yoga involves stretching, relaxation and breath control. It is a good way of improving posture, breathing and suppleness.

For information about local classes, write to Extend, 22 Maltings Drive, Wheathampstead, Herts AL4 8QJ. Tel: 01582 832760.

Exercising at home

If you don't like the idea of joining a class, you can exercise at home, to the accompaniment of a cassette, video or keep-fit programme on television.

If you are contemplating buying an exercise machine, an exercise bike is useful and versatile though many people get bored with them and find they hardly ever use them. It is worth checking that it is stable, avoiding a machine that rocks as you use it. Step machines simulate stair climbing. Hydraulic resistance cushions each step you take and prevents strain on knees.

You can also try to include more exercise in your daily life by walking or cycling rather than taking the bus or car, walking up stairs in shops and offices rather than using escalators or lifts, and so on.

Eating well

There is no shortage of leaflets and posters telling us the kinds of foods we should be eating. Much has been written recently about the values of the traditional Mediterranean diet, based largely on pasta, vegetables and olive oil. We are probably all aware that we should as a nation be reducing fat, sugar and salt in our diet and eating more fibre-rich foods and more fruit and vegetables.

This does not mean that we have all followed this advice and made the necessary changes – although many people have made changes in their eating habits in recent years.

Less fat

A small amount of fat in the diet is essential but most of us should eat less of it. Eating less fat has two main advantages:

▶ As fat is extremely high in calories, it will help you lose weight if you need to.

▶ Cutting down on saturated fats – mainly animal fats – reduces the level of cholesterol in the blood and so lessens the risk of coronary heart disease.

We are therefore advised to grill rather than fry, trim all visible fat from meat, use all fats sparingly, and switch to semi-skimmed or skimmed milk and low-fat products. When we do fry food, an oil that is high in unsaturates such as olive oil or sunflower oil is recommended. Remember that there is hidden fat in foods such as crisps, cakes and chocolate.

At the same time we are told to eat more oily fish, which is rich in polyunsaturates and other nutritional elements that are thought to be beneficial. These are believed to help reduce the tendency of the blood to clot, so lessening the risk of thrombosis and heart attacks.

Less sugar

For people who love chocolate, cakes and biscuits, cutting down on sugar is not easy, but the advantages are all too obvious:

▶ As sugar is high in calories, it will help weight loss if this is needed. The calories that sugar provides are 'empty' ones: sugar contains calories but has no food value.

▶ Sugar is a prime cause of tooth decay and gum disease.

Much of the sugar we eat is hidden in that it is added to foods such as baked beans and breakfast cereals. It is worth checking on food labels to see whether sugar has been added and how much (ingredients are always listed in order of quantity).

Less salt

Although the links between large amounts of salt in the diet and high blood pressure have not been proved conclusively, it is recommended that people should cut down their consumption of salt as much as they possibly can.

Cut down on salt by reducing gradually the amount used in cooking or sprinkled on food. Herbs and spices reduce the need for salt. Cutting down on salty snacks and preserved foods such as bacon, ham and sausages will also help. Other salty foods used in cooking are stock cubes and soy sauce.

More fibre

Wholemeal bread, wholegrain breakfast cereals, beans, lentils, fruit and vegetables are rich in fibre. There are two types of fibre, both vitally important:

▶ The type which predominates in cereals is needed to keep the bowel system working and avoid constipation.

▶ The type which predominates in beans, oats, fruit and vegetables may help correct blood cholesterol levels.

It is currently said that most people in Britain need to increase their intake of fibre by eating more fruit and vegetables and more starchy foods such as bread, cereals, pasta, potatoes and rice. These foods are a good source of energy and an essential part of a balanced diet.

Vitamins and minerals

Vitamin and mineral supplements will not usually be necessary if you:

▶ eat a variety of foods, including plenty of fruit and vegetables;

▶ ensure that the food you eat is fresh – storing food properly will help keep it fresh;

▶ do not overcook vegetables – cook for a short time in as little water as possible.

Fluids

The body needs three to four pints of fluid a day in order to function properly. In particular, constipation can be aggravated by not drinking enough.

Alcohol

Alcohol is part of many people's eating and drinking pattern and is fine in moderation. The average recommended guidelines for weekly alcohol consumption are 14–21 units for women and 21–28 for men, spread through the week. (Half a pint of beer, lager or cider, one small glass of wine, sherry or port, or one measure of spirits all comprise one unit.) However, these limits may be too high as you get older, as tolerance of alcohol seems to decrease with age.

While drinking too much can raise blood pressure and eventually cause liver damage, people who drink small amounts of alcohol regularly – perhaps 1–2 units a day – are less likely to develop coronary heart disease.

 For confidential information, help and advice about drinking telephone Drinkline – London: 0171-332 0202. All UK: 0345 32 02 02. AsianLine (Dial & Listen) 0990 133 480 in Hindu, Gujarati and Urdu.

Avoiding food poisoning

There have been many alarms about the safety of particular foods in recent years, and records indicate that food poisoning is on the increase.

SALMONELLA The most common cause of food poisoning is probably salmonella bacteria, particularly associated with poultry and eggs. The bacteria are killed when food is thoroughly cooked. When cooking or reheating it is therefore vital that foods are heated until they are piping hot (over 70°C throughout).

This should not present a problem with poultry, which is always served cooked right through, but eggs are often served lightly cooked, as in scrambled eggs, or even raw, as in chocolate mousse. If you fall into one of the Department of Health's 'at risk' categories, you should avoid lightly cooked or raw eggs.

The 'at risk' categories include frail elderly people, people who are ill or convalescent, and people with a reduced resistance to infection, either because they are taking medicines which suppress the body's natural immunity or because of a condition such as AIDS or diabetes.

Another useful precaution is to ensure that raw eggs and poultry do not contaminate other food. It is a good idea to keep raw poultry at the bottom of the fridge to make sure it does not drip on to other foods, and to make sure chopping boards and utensils are cleaned thoroughly.

LISTERIA There is only a very small risk of a healthy person contracting listeriosis. However, listeria bacteria can continue to multiply at fridge temperature, so it is wise for anyone in an 'at risk' category to avoid all foods likely to contain high levels of the bacteria. These include:

▶ raw unpasteurised milk;

▶ soft mould-ripened cheese such as Brie, Camembert and Danish blue;

▶ pre-cooked chiller meals and roasted poultry;

▶ meat, fish or vegetable pâté;

▶ soft-whip ice cream from machines.

E COLI While forms of *E coli* are found naturally in the human gut, the lethal form that led to the food poisoning outbreak in 1996–97 occurs mainly in beef. As with salmonella, the bacteria are killed by thorough cooking, especially important with all forms of minced beef, hamburgers, etc. As mentioned above, it is a good idea to keep raw meat at the bottom of the fridge and to be scrupulous about cleaning knives and chopping boards.

See Age Concern Books' *Eating Well on a Budget* for more tips about safe handling and storing of food, and for a week's lunch and supper recipes for each season of the year. *Healthy Eating on a Budget* explains the principles of healthy eating and provides over 100 healthy and delicious recipes (details on p 201).

Impurities in water

Recently much anxiety has been expressed about the purity of tap water, which is liable to be contaminated by a variety of chemicals and heavy metals which are considered dangerous.

Water companies are supposed to be building more sensitive filtration plants in order to meet European standards, and Government scientists assure us that contaminants in tap water are now at safe levels. Nevertheless an increasing number of people now use home filter systems. Filters are currently of two types:

PLUMBED-IN FILTERS, which cost up to several hundred pounds.

JUG FILTERS, which treat only small amounts of water. The jug is cheap but the filters, which need to be changed monthly, are comparatively expensive. Check what percentage of pollutants each brand of filter claims to remove. Electronic jug filters are more expensive to buy initially, but they remove a large percentage of pollutants, have a longer-life cartridge, and will remove the problem of limescale in hard-water areas.

Pesticides

Concern is also expressed about pesticide residues in food. The newer pesticides now in use remain in the environment for shorter periods than earlier ones, and residue levels are thought to be low.

Careful washing or peeling removes some pesticides, but not systemic pesticides that are absorbed by the cells of the plant. If you want to avoid residues it is best to buy organic food, grown without any deliberate application of pesticides.

Losing weight

Being overweight when you're older increases the risk of diabetes, high blood pressure, heart disease and varicose veins and puts additional stress on your joints, particularly knees and hips.

Being overweight is the result of an imbalance between calorie intake and energy output. Eating fewer calories and doing more exercise should help. The easiest way to take in fewer calories is to follow the basic principles of healthy eating: less fat, sugar and salt and more fibre-rich foods.

OUTSIDE HELP WITH WEIGHT LOSS Be wary of any organisation that advertises rapid weight loss through special diets or diet foods. What you should be aiming for is permanent weight loss, which can come about only through a change in your energy needs or eating habits.

WEIGHT WATCHERS offer group support and regular weight checks. They have three diet levels, depending how fast you want to lose weight; they also have a vegetarian diet and an exercise plan.

 For the address of your nearest Weight Watchers group, contact Weight Watchers (UK) Ltd, Kidwells Park House, Kidwells Park Drive, Maidenhead, Berkshire SL6 8YT. Tel: 01628 777077.

 If you are interested in getting together in a group with other older people for health-related activities, Age Concern England's *Age Well Handbook* and *Age Well Planning and Ideas Pack* (details on p 204) provide a step-by-step guide to setting up such groups.

Smoking

It has long been known that smoking causes lung cancer, coronary heart disease, chronic bronchitis and emphysema. It is now recognised that it is also a cause of strokes, arteriosclerosis (the build-up of fatty tissues and loss of elasticity in the arteries) and other cancers, including cancer of the mouth, and that it is a contributory factor in yet more diseases. It also affects your general fitness and makes you more inclined to get out of breath.

Giving up will benefit your health whatever your age, however long you have been smoking, and whether you smoke cigarettes, cigars or a pipe.

After 10–15 years an ex-smoker's risk of developing lung cancer is only slightly greater than that of someone who has never smoked, and the relative risk of a heart attack is reduced almost to that of a non-smoker.

FACTFILE

▶ Smoking is the most important cause of preventable disease and early death in the UK.

▶ Each year about 111,000 people die as a result of their smoking.

▶ 10 million people in the UK have stopped smoking – and stayed stopped – in the last ten years. That's 1,000 people each day.

▶ 29 per cent of people in their 50s smoke, but less than 20 per cent of people aged 60 or over.

Within a few weeks your hair, skin and breath will stop smelling of tobacco smoke and your breathing will improve, as will your sense of taste and smell.

The best way is usually to give up completely rather than trying to cut down gradually. It may help to analyse when you smoke. If you smoke after meals, for example, try to break the habit by washing the dishes or going for a walk before you reach for a cigarette. Any withdrawal symptoms will usually have gone in a month, probably less.

Getting help

If you feel you need outside help, there is plenty available – consult your GP for advice and information.

▶ Quitline is a national telephone helpline for smokers who need advice or help in stopping – dial Freephone 0800 00 22 00. They will give you details of your nearest stop-smoking group and can send you an information Quitpack.

▶ Acupuncture or hypnosis is found helpful by some people, but such treatment is generally only available privately and may be expensive.

Dental care

Gone are the days when everyone expected to lose all their own teeth and wear dentures instead. Improvements in dental techniques mean that it is now possible to fill or crown almost any tooth. Teeth are more likely to be lost through advanced gum disease, which is much more difficult to treat.

Gum disease is caused by ineffective cleaning of the teeth, leaving plaque in the areas where teeth and gums meet. Bacteria in plaque 'feed' off the food we eat and produce waste products which cause inflammation of the gums and eventually loosening of the teeth. The first sign of gum disease is when gums bleed easily.

Receding of the gums due to gum disease cannot be reversed, but it can be halted. To prevent gum disease and tooth decay:

- ▶ Brush teeth thoroughly daily with a medium-texture, small-headed brush – dentists suggest this should take at least five minutes.
- ▶ Use dental floss or wooden dental sticks – you can ask your dentist or hygienist for advice.
- ▶ Use a toothpaste containing fluoride.
- ▶ Cut down your intake of sugar, which converts into acid in the mouth and attacks your teeth. To cut down the number of times you eat sugar, dentists usually recommend that you keep sugar-containing foods to meal times.
- ▶ Go to your dentist for a check-up at least once a year.

Denture problems

It is a good idea to go to a dentist once a year even if you have none of your own teeth left. Gums naturally change shape when the teeth have been removed, at first rapidly and then more slowly, so dentures need to be adjusted and sometimes replaced. The discomfort many people report with their dentures may well be because they are wearing ill-fitting or broken dentures that should have been replaced years ago.

Brushing dentures properly is extremely important: plaque builds up on dentures as well as on teeth, and can cause the tissues underneath to become infected. When you take your dentures out you should always keep them wet: if the plastic is allowed to dry out, the dentures may warp.

Obtaining dental care

Since October 1990 there has been a new system of dental care. It is a good idea to make sure you are registered with a dentist for 'continuing care' (regular treatment). This entitles you to all the care and treatment you need to maintain oral health, and emergency dental treatment if necessary.

Before each course of treatment, the patient and dentist should discuss any treatment that is proposed and what it will cost. The dentist will usually draw up a 'treatment plan'; if this doesn't happen, you can always ask for one.

Continuing care arrangements between patient and dentist last 15 months and can then be renewed. You can sign on with any dentist you like provided they are taking NHS patients and are willing to accept you.

 For a list of NHS dentists in your area, contact your local Health Authority. The list should also be available at main post offices and libraries and at the Community Health Council.

Paying for dental care

You will generally pay 80 per cent of the costs of all treatment, up to a ceiling of £330 for any one course of treatment (1997 figure). If you are on Income Support or income-based Jobseeker's Allowance or have a low income you may be entitled to free treatment or some help with the costs, as explained on page 24.

There are no set fees for private treatment, nor is there any help towards private dental fees from NHS sources.

For more information about dental care, see Age Concern Factsheet 5 *Dental care in retirement.*

Looking after your feet

A great many adults have foot problems, often as a result of wearing ill-fitting shoes. It makes sense to start looking after your feet from now on: they may have to last you for another 30 years or so, and if they are not in good shape it will be harder for you to remain active as you get older.

To help keep your feet in good condition:

- ▶ Wash them daily, making sure you dry them thoroughly.
- ▶ Remove any build-up of hard skin with a pumice stone.
- ▶ Rub in cream, exercising your toes as you do so.
- ▶ Exercise your ankles by rotating your feet, one at a time, first in a clockwise and then in an anti-clockwise direction.

CUTTING YOUR TOE NAILS Toe nails dry out and become harder to cut as you get older. Immediately after washing is a good time to cut them as the water makes them softer. An alternative is to file them with an emery board. Always consult a chiropodist if you have painful or ingrowing toe nails.

ACHING FEET If your feet are aching and swollen at the end of the day, it may help to lie or sit down with your feet raised higher than your hips for about 15 minutes. Dipping tired feet alternately, for a minute at a time, in warm and then cold water will help the circulation. Try not to sit with your legs or ankles crossed for too much of the time, as this restricts the circulation.

INFLAMED, SWOLLEN OR PAINFUL FEET You should consult a doctor if any part of your foot becomes inflamed, swollen or painful or if the skin becomes white, dusky red or purple, because the blood circulation to the foot may be affected.

CORNS AND CALLUSES It is advisable to have these treated by a chiropodist, particularly if you have circulation problems or a condition such as diabetes which leaves you more prone to infections.

NHS CHIROPODY SERVICES are free to anyone over the age of 60, but the extent of provision varies in different parts of the country. If there is a delay in being seen you may want to consider private treatment. The NHS employs only state-registered chiropodists, who use the letters SRCh after their names.

 For guidance on foot conditions, and adapting shoes for comfort, see Age Concern Books' *The Foot Care Book* (details on p 202).

Skin care

Various factors will affect the quality of your skin as you get older:

▶ People with oily skins tend to develop fewer wrinkles.

▶ Smokers tend to have more.

▶ People who have lived in a sunny climate or worked outdoors will tend to have tanned, leathery skin.

▶ People who are on the plump side will usually show fewer signs of ageing.

In addition, many people's skin suffers from neglect. If you have very dry skin, a vegetable-based soap and regular moisturiser will help. Moisturiser will also help keep the skin supple. If you use foundation cream, it is a good tip to put moisturiser on first.

Be wary of advertisements for skin products that make such promises as 'Within days you will look younger' or 'Put the brakes on the ageing process'. These are basically just an effective way of persuading people to part with their money. In the United States, where consumers are far better protected than here, cosmetics companies have been forced to withdraw such claims.

 Avon Cosmetics sells its products in people's homes or you can order products over the phone. For a brochure or the name and address of the local representative, phone them on Freephone 0800 663 664.

If you are interested in cosmetics that are unlikely to cause an allergic reaction, Almay Cosmetics has a range of products. For names of stockists and advice on products, contact their Customer Services Department on 0171-491 5450.

Advice on camouflage creams to hide skin blemishes is available from the British Red Cross. They also use volunteers to teach blind and partially sighted women to apply make-up. Enquire from your local branch first before contacting the London office at 9 Grosvenor Crescent, London SW1X 7EJ. Tel: 0171-235 5454.

Dealing with hair loss

While many men suffer what is known as pattern baldness – a receding hairline and thinning on the crown – women may experience overall thinning. Some people with thinning hair may find a change of hairstyle helps, but others may consider more radical solutions.

Hair replacement

There are many different methods of hair replacement, surgical and non-surgical. Impartial advice can be obtained from a qualified trichologist.

The drug Minoxidil represents the most promising breakthrough to date in the search for a cure for baldness, but it is successful only in some cases. It is worth consulting a trichologist to see whether it is likely to be helpful to you.

Another problem is that if you stop taking it your hair will revert very quickly to how it would have been at that point if you had never taken the drug. You may therefore find yourself committed to using it for life, at around £25 a month (1997 prices). You can buy it over the counter as Regaine or you can get a stronger dosage on prescription, but it is unlikely to be available on the NHS.

Wigs, toupées and hairpieces

A wig can be a major asset to anyone who experiences sudden hair loss. This can occur at any age and is always very distressing. It is often a side-effect of chemotherapy, but it can be due to shock, a scalp disorder or another medical condition. In addition, both men and women with thinning hair can change their appearance dramatically by wearing a wig or toupée.

Today's wigs and hairpieces are lightweight, with mesh linings to allow for easy air circulation, so they do not damage the scalp or the natural hair. Wigs made from carefully matched human hair are the best, but they are expensive and need a lot of maintenance. Acrylic fibre wigs are cheaper, lighter and easier to look after at home.

 For general advice on hair and scalp problems write to the Institute of Trichologists. They can send you a list of registered member trichologists in your area; they also publish several leaflets, including one on general hair care and another on consulting a trichologist. Write to them at 20–22 Queensberry Place, London SW7 2DZ, enclosing an sae.

Sexuality and relationships

It is all too easy to get the impression from TV, films and advertising that sex is only for the young and beautiful – beauty being identified with being slim, lithe and unwrinkled. While older people are encouraged to take up new interests which will be intellectually stimulating, there is still almost a taboo on translating that into the development of personal relationships and the realms of sexual exploration. In fact many couples enjoy sex more as they get older, finding this aspect of their lives rewarding and fulfilling and just as important to them as to younger couples.

Sex and older people

Sexual behaviour varies considerably over time among couples of all ages. Sometimes sex is passionate, sometimes it is calmer and quieter. At times it may become less important or even burdensome – desire can be affected by a range of factors, from physical health and emotional well-being to worries about family, work or money.

Most people are able to enjoy some form of sexual love throughout their lives, but our sexuality may not always be expressed in the same way. For some older people, orgasm may become less frequent and less intense; the shared intimacy of body contact, of lying next to each other, of stroking, touching, caressing and being held, may become more important than actual intercourse.

Growing older may in fact bring some very real advantages as far as our sexual lives are concerned:

▶ Once women are past the menopause both they and their partners can enjoy love-making without contraceptives and without fear of an unwanted pregnancy.

- ► For many older women the fact that their partner now takes longer to reach a climax makes love-making far more enjoyable than before.
- ► When people retire they may have more time and energy for sex and sexual exploration and find their sex lives actually improve.

Improving your sex life

For some older couples sexual intercourse becomes increasingly infrequent; eventually they give it up entirely. Often the main reason is boredom: the same thing done in the same way at the same time in the same place tends to become boring for anyone. Women who grew up before the Second World War were often not taught to expect any pleasure from sex; as a result many have never enjoyed it and may be relieved to give it up altogether. Men may be unimaginative in their love-making, partly because they too expect women to be passive and unresponsive.

Anyone who harbours even the slightest feeling that older people should not really have sexual desires may feel uneasy, even guilty, at the idea of sexual exploration. This may be even more the case for people who are attracted to people of their own sex. This is a pity because there are many ways in which people, young and old, whatever their sexual orientation, can attempt to improve their sex lives.

Talking about what you want

Most of us find it hard to talk about sex, even to our partners of many years' standing. Yet the fact that someone cares for us does not mean that they will automatically know what we want and when, what we like and don't like. If partners are expected to guess, it is not surprising that they sometimes guess wrong. Learning to communicate what we want, either in words or by our actions, and in turn becoming more attuned to our partner's needs, can improve and enrich our love lives immensely.

Trying something new

Many couples have only used one or two positions for intercourse throughout their married life – most common is probably the missionary position, in which the man lies on top of the woman – but trying different positions can in itself produce new sensations.

Perhaps one of the problems is that many couples regard sex as an almost entirely genital activity. Yet people often like to spend time kissing and caressing before any genital contact is made, and some prefer non-penetrative sex or enjoy a great deal of manual stimulation of the genitals before intercourse – some women may only reach orgasm this way.

Some couples might feel curious about oral sex but feel inhibited about trying it. The fact that it is sometimes regarded as almost a perversion may make it harder to accept that it is perfectly normal.

Factfile

- ▶ In 1995 17 per cent of men and 36 per cent of women in the 65–74 age group lived alone.

- ▶ These percentages rose to 33 per cent and 62 per cent for men and women aged 75 or over.

- ▶ In 1994 75 per cent of men in Great Britain in the 65–74 age group were married, compared to 51 per cent of women.

The same is true of sex aids such as vibrators and dildos. Until recently often considered as unnatural, even 'kinky', they too can enhance love-making and help partners give each other maximum satisfaction. Watching explicit movies together can also be stimulating and arouse sexual feelings. Anyone, regardless of age, should feel free to try anything that they and their partner feel happy about.

A complete change of scene can also be exciting – going to bed and making love during the day, making love in a different room in the house. One of the bonuses of retirement is that this is so much more possible. Having a special supper together – either at home or in a restaurant – can reintroduce the romantic element which may have disappeared from our lives. Watching a film or having a bath together can be a good prelude to going to bed. Finally, a short trip away from home can give a couple a chance to rediscover their enjoyment of each other.

Sensate focusing

Sensate focusing is a form of sex therapy; it was pioneered by Masters and Johnson in the United States and is sometimes known by their names. It is particularly suitable for couples who are having arousal problems such as frigidity or impotence or an inability to enjoy sex in that it concentrates on each partner giving and receiving pleasure rather than worrying about sexual intercourse and reaching a climax.

The treatment consists of three separate phases, which may last several weeks each. During the first phase, the couple are told to stroke each other's bodies, apart from the genitals, telling each other what they like and don't like. At this stage most therapists recommend that there should be no sexual intercourse, however much the couple desire it. At the next stage genital stimulation is also allowed, with the couple again telling each other what they like and don't like. Finally, they go on to full intercourse.

For information about the availability of sexual and marital therapy, both NHS and private sector, send an sae to the Bufill Association of Sexual and Marital Therapists, PO Box 62, Sheffield S10 3TS.

The Association to Aid the Sexual and Personal Relationships of People with a Disability (SPOD), 286 Camden Road, London N7 0BJ. Tel: 0171-607 8851, provides an advisory and counselling service for people with disabilities who are having sexual difficulties.

Sexual problems

Sexual problems can arise for many reasons – because of a medical condition, after an operation, because of the circumstances in which a couple live, or for reasons that are more explicitly sexual, such as anxiety about performance.

It seems that couples sometimes stop having sex altogether because of a specific difficulty, which they may attribute to ageing. But such difficulties can usually be overcome, and sexual activity be resumed.

ARTHRITIS can make sex painful. In particular, arthritis of the hip can make it difficult for a woman to open her legs, making intercourse with the woman lying on her back impossible. One solution is for the woman to lie on her side, with the man lying behind her 'like a pair of spoons'. The use of pillows to support and cushion painful limbs may be helpful, as may an extra dose of painkiller, preferably before foreplay begins. (See pp 158–159 for more about arthritis.)

DRUGS can affect sexual performance and enjoyment. If this is reported to the doctor, the treatment can sometimes be changed. Doctors should always tell patients of possible side-effects so that they can make an informed choice about their own treatment.

INCONTINENCE affects a great many older people (see pp 164–165) and can be embarrassing if it occurs during intercourse. One solution is to empty the bladder immediately before starting to make love and to avoid drinking in the two to three hours before bedtime.

BREATHLESSNESS, A HEART ATTACK OR A STROKE may all make it necessary to use techniques that reduce the effort involved: love-making should be as gentle and undemanding as possible. The affected partner should avoid taking too active a role, and might try being propped up in bed or sitting up on a chair rather than lying flat. Non-penetrative sex might sometimes be better than full intercourse.

DEPRESSION often causes a loss of sexual desire. Many people see this as a symptom of ageing rather than of an illness which can be cured, by drugs or counselling or a mixture of the two.

OPERATIONS can leave older people feeling very low, and they are often afraid that sex will be harmful. Patients and their partners should be fully informed about what to expect before the operation, and offered help with any difficulties afterwards, including advice as to when it is safe to resume sexual activity. Prostate operations for men, and mastectomy and hysterectomy operations for women, may be particularly traumatic. There are specially trained nurses who help people who have had a colostomy operation.

LACK OF PRIVACY may put people off making love, for example if a couple live in their children's home and cannot lock the bedroom door, or if children are in the habit of entering their parents' home without knocking.

VAGINAL DRYNESS AND TIGHTNESS may be a problem for some women after the menopause. This can be overcome by the use of KY jelly or any contraceptive cream, and in the longer term possibly by hormone replacement therapy (HRT – see p 166).

SEXUAL PERFORMANCE is a problem for many men. Impotence, total or partial (when the penis never becomes very hard), can be caused by a physical disease, by the fact that older men have less of the hormone testosterone than when they were younger, or by anxiety about performing satisfactorily. Problems can be helped by counselling and sensate focusing, or by the use of penile rings (available from sex shops and some chemists), injections or penile implants.

GENERAL PROBLEMS WITHIN A RELATIONSHIP can also cause sexual difficulties. The reality of retirement often does not match up to people's expectations, and couples may find it difficult to adjust to suddenly having so much more time together. Good retirement courses can help a couple talk about their hopes and fears. Couples who need help in working through their problems could see a counsellor. Counsellors may be attached to doctors' surgeries, or you may be able to see one through Relate (formerly the National Marriage Guidance Council).

 For the address of your nearest Relate branch, either look in your local phone book or contact Relate, Herbert Gray College, Little Church Street, Rugby, Warwickshire CV21 3AP. Tel: 01788 573241.

People on their own

Although having a partner is by no means an automatic solution to all life's problems, there are certain things it does make easier. You have someone to go on holiday with, to go to the cinema with, to share both your major worries and your day-to-day experiences. You also have someone – potentially at least – to satisfy your sexual needs.

Many people were brought up to regard masturbation as sinful, and some still feel guilty about it. Yet everyone has some sexual needs, and satisfying those needs is just one more thing that people on their own have to do for themselves. Many single people find the use of sex aids such as a vibrator helpful.

Finding a new partner

Many people on their own hope that they will find a new partner. This is particularly difficult for older women: not only are they far more numerous than older men, but men of their own age are often looking for much younger partners. Older men, on the other hand, find themselves outnumbered by women almost everywhere they go.

Many people find that the opportunities for meeting new people are few and far between, especially once they have left work and their children have left home. Starting new activities outside the home – joining a club or society, going to an evening class, doing some voluntary work – can all help. Another option is to go to a dating agency or marriage bureau, of which there are many.

People go to marriage bureaux for many different reasons. Some want a long-term relationship – someone to live with or marry. Others seek only companionship and a friend to see two or three times a week, and perhaps to go on holiday with. For some people, sex will be an important part of any such relationship; for others it will be less important or even unwanted. Anyone who goes to a marriage bureau should be as clear as possible about what they want and what they do not want. They should also try to find out from the people they meet what they want from the relationship.

When we talk about sexual experience and finding a new partner, we tend to think of love between a man and a woman, but it could also be love between two people of the same sex. Many people are capable of both heterosexual and homosexual love: someone who was happily married for years may find that a close friendship with someone of their own sex can include warmth and physical affection, and even extend to a close sexual relationship.

 For more about sexuality and relationships as we get older, see Age Concern Books' *Living, Loving and Ageing* (details on p 201).

Health problems

Most people are likely to stay fit and active well into their 80s. Some may encounter new health concerns, such as high blood pressure or heart disease, and have to watch what they eat to a greater extent than before or take exercise more regularly. With a little care, most such conditions need not be a bar to a fulfilling lifestyle. This section looks at some of the more common health problems that can affect people as they get older, with the emphasis always on preventive measures and positive ways of coping. If you want more information, there are many organisations that offer advice and information about specific illnesses and disabilities.

Arthritis

There are three main types of arthritis: rheumatoid arthritis, which can come on in middle age; osteoarthritis, which is common in old age; and gout, which – contrary to popular belief – is not caused by excessive drinking.

Preventive measures

Joints are damaged by arthritis, but you can help prevent further injury by:

▶ keeping your weight down, thus reducing the pressure on joints;

▶ keeping yourself mobile;

▶ exercising as much as possible without straining a painful joint.

Swimming is particularly good, as is cycling, provided the arthritis is not too severe. Exercise which jolts the joints such as jogging or aerobics should be avoided.

Alleviating pain

There are various things you can do to try to ease aching, painful joints:

▶ Rest a painful joint, especially after standing for long periods. Balance rest with activity – too much rest can cause muscle stiffness.

▶ Keep the affected area warm with a covered hot water bottle or heat pad.

▶ Take painkillers – but you should consult a doctor if you need to take them more than once or twice a week.

> **FACTFILE**
>
> ▶ In 1995 63 per cent of people aged 75 or over had a long-standing illness, compared to 31 per cent of people of all ages.
>
> ▶ Of these, 48 per cent said they had a long-standing illness that limited their lifestyle.

In severe cases the doctor may arrange physiotherapy, or replacement of the damaged joint with an artificial one. Hip replacements are now common and safe, and knee replacements increasingly so.

 For more information contact Arthritis Care, 18 Stephenson Way, London NW1 2HD. Their helpline is open weekdays 12–4pm on Freephone 0800 289 170.

For advice on equipment and clothing specially designed for people with arthritic hands and other joint problems, write to the Disabled Living Foundation, 380–384 Harrow Road, London W9 2HU.

 For more information about aids and adaptations in the home for people with disabilities, see pages 170–173.

Cancer

A diagnosis of cancer should not be regarded as an automatic death sentence: if diagnosed and treated early enough, many cancers can be completely cured. Sadly, many people do not report symptoms until the cancer is far advanced. Symptoms that should be reported to a doctor immediately include:

► passing blood, in vomit, sputum, faeces or urine, or from the vagina;

► unexplained weight loss or loss of appetite;

► hoarseness that persists for more than two weeks or a persistent cough;

► persistent indigestion or difficulty in swallowing;

► an unusual lump in the breast or armpit or a change in the shape or size of the breast or in the colour of the nipple;

► a sore on the lips, tongue or face that does not heal or is getting bigger;

► lumps or tenderness in the testicles, or difficulty passing urine, which can all be signs of prostate cancer;

► a mole that is itching, inflamed, bleeding or crusting, or growing in size, which can be a sign of skin cancer;

► an unexplained change in bowel habits.

As there are several hundred different types of cancer, this list is by no means comprehensive.

All women should be screened for cervical cancer by means of a smear test every three to five years. Women between 50 and 64 are also entitled to a free mammography (breast X-ray) every three years. Screening is generally organised by your GP.

 For information and advice contact CancerLink, 11–21 Northdown Street, London N1 9BN. Tel: 0171-833 2818.

For information, advice and counselling about breast cancer or other breast-related problems, contact Breast Cancer Care, Kiln House, 210 New Kings Road, London SW6 4NZ. Freephone 0500 245 345.

Diabetes

Diabetes often develops in older people when the pancreas fails to produce enough insulin or the insulin it does produce cannot work properly. Insulin is needed to help the body use sugar to produce energy.

Some people suffer the symptoms of diabetes – including tiredness, blurred vision, weight changes, thirst and passing water more frequently than usual – but put them down to other things. If you think you might have diabetes, your doctor can do a simple on-the-spot blood or urine test.

There is no cure for diabetes but it can be successfully treated. The type of diabetes that commonly develops in older people does not usually require insulin but can be controlled by cutting down the amount of sugar and carbohydrate in your diet, with the advice of your GP or local health centre.

If diet is not enough alone, your doctor may prescribe tablets or another form of insulin to control your diabetes.

If you have diabetes, you should pay particular attention to foot care, as minor cuts or abrasions can lead to a serious infection. It is advisable to visit a chiropodist regularly for a check-up. As a diabetic, you will be entitled to free sight tests. It is very important that you have an annual medical examination which includes a check on eyesight and an examination of the back of the eye.

For information and advice about diabetes, including a wide range of leaflets, contact the British Diabetic Association, 10 Queen Anne Street, London W1M 0BD. Careline: 0171-636 6112 weekdays 9am–5pm.

Eye problems

As you grow older, the lens of the eye tends to lose its elasticity; as a result older people often need glasses for reading. This is a normal change.

In addition, some older people develop one of three common eye diseases:

▶ cataract (a clouding of the lens);

▶ glaucoma (when the fluid inside the eyeball increases);

▶ macular degeneration (which affects the retina).

Diabetes can also impair your sight. Cataract and glaucoma are both treatable, and laser treatment can often halt the changes that occur in diabetes.

You should have a sight test every year, and sooner if you notice changes in your eyesight. Opticians may now charge for a sight test, but you will be entitled to a free one if you are in a priority group or if you are on Income Support or income-based Jobseeker's Allowance.

 For details about help with the cost of sight tests and glasses for people with low incomes, see page 24.

Hearing problems

Some loss of ability to hear high-pitched sounds, such as the telephone, is common as people get older. If you are unable to follow a conversation with several people talking, or experience other problems with your hearing, consult your GP.

FACTFILE

Of people aged 65 or over:

▶ At least one-third have hearing difficulties, and one in ten has a hearing aid.

▶ 23 per cent have a hearing difficulty but no hearing aid.

▶ 97 per cent wear glasses.

▶ 20 per cent have difficulty seeing even with their glasses.

If hearing difficulties are not due to wax in the ear or an ear infection, your GP may refer you to a hearing aid centre or a hospital ear, nose and throat (ENT) clinic. NHS hearing aids are available on free loan; replacements and batteries are also free. Initially some people dislike the way hearing aids amplify background sounds as well as what they actually want to hear, but it is usually worth persevering.

If you want information about tinnitus (ringing in the ears) or other hearing problems, contact the Royal National Institute for Deaf People, 19–23 Featherstone Street, London EC1Y 8SL. Tel: 0171-296 8000.

Heart disease

Heart disease usually develops before people are 65, although symptoms may not appear until later, so prevention should start much earlier. To reduce the likelihood of heart disease developing, or to prevent an already existing heart condition getting worse, there are various things you can do:

► Stop smoking.

► Keep your weight steady, or lose some if you are overweight.

► Reduce your overall intake of fat and switch to more unsaturated fats.

► Take exercise – swimming and walking are ideal, but be guided by your doctor.

Some heart conditions can be controlled by drugs, which your GP will advise you about. For long-term treatment, various heart operations are now common.

 For further information contact the British Heart Foundation, 14 Fitzhardinge Street, London W1H 4DH. Tel: 0171-935 0185.

High blood pressure

People with high blood pressure, or hypertension, may feel perfectly well and experience no symptoms, but statistics show that they are far more likely to develop certain vascular diseases – stroke, heart failure, coronary thrombosis or kidney failure – than people with lower blood pressure. The object of treating hypertension is therefore to prevent vascular disease and enable you to lead a full and active life without placing yourself at any special risk.

Most people with high blood pressure need to take some form of medication. However, there are certain things you can do yourself to help lower blood pressure:

▶ Lose weight if you are overweight.

▶ Eat less salt.

▶ Give up smoking and limit your alcohol intake.

▶ Avoid stress.

▶ Consult your doctor about whether exercise might help.

Incontinence

Although incontinence is common among older people, it is not a 'normal' part of ageing. Many types of incontinence can be treated or cured. That is why it is so important to overcome the inhibitions some people feel about talking about such personal matters, and find out why you, or the person you care for, has a problem.

STRESS INCONTINENCE – leaking of urine when you laugh, cough or sneeze – is mainly experienced by women. It can be caused by stretching of the pelvic floor muscles during childbirth or by hormonal changes following the menopause. This can be cured completely and quickly by exercises to strengthen the pelvic muscles.

To feel your pelvic muscles, imagine you are trying to control diarrhoea by tightening the muscles round the back passage. Then imagine you are trying to stop passing urine by tightening the muscles around the outlet from the bladder. Slowly tighten the pelvic muscles, working from back to front, to a slow count of four, then gently let go. Repeat four times. These exercises can be done sitting, standing or lying down. You should do them at least four times a day: the more often, the sooner you will feel the benefit.

FREQUENCY OR URGENCY – needing to pass urine very frequently or experiencing a sudden very strong urge to do so – may be caused by an infection or other problems, so consult your doctor. Bladder training may help: when you want to pass urine urgently, practise holding on, first for a minute, then gradually for longer.

LEAKING or dribbling is more common in men, often caused by prostate problems. It can also be caused by constipation, which can cause pressure on the bladder. Consult your doctor.

Whatever form of incontinence you suffer from, it is important to keep as active as possible, eat lots of fibre and drink plenty. This will help prevent constipation, which can lead to both bladder and bowel problems.

It is also worth making sure that you, or the person you are caring for, go to the toilet regularly. If you have an older relative in a residential home who suffers from incontinence, you should check that there are enough toilets, that people are helped to go to the toilet at regular intervals, and that clothing can be unfastened easily.

If incontinence is to be successfully treated, the first step is accurate diagnosis. Always consult your doctor. He or she should be able to help, but there may also be a specially trained continence adviser in your area – check with your GP or health visitor. The continence adviser should be able to identify the cause of incontinence and suggest appropriate treatment, whether in the form of exercise, medication or other treatments. He or she will also be able to give advice on the wide range of products and equipment available to help cope with incontinence.

 For more information and advice, phone the Continence Helpline on 0191-213 0050, weekdays 9am–6pm. They will also be able to give you the name of your local continence adviser.

 Age Concern Factsheet 23 *Help with incontinence* includes many useful addresses and publications, while Age Concern Books' *In Control* (details on p 202) gives more detailed information about the causes and treatment of incontinence.

Osteoporosis

Osteoporosis causes bones to become so porous and fragile that they break very easily. Thousands of older women suffer painful and deforming fractures – of hips, wrists and spine – and men can be affected too.

After the menopause, as the oestrogen level in women's bodies declines, women begin to lose bone from their skeleton, sometimes gradually and sometimes very rapidly. Those particularly at risk include:

▶ women who have had an early menopause or hysterectomy;

▶ women who have over-dieted or suffered anorexia or bulimia nervosa, as their calcium intake may have been very low;

▶ women who have over-exercised or who have missed a lot of periods for other reasons;

▶ men or women who have already had a fracture after a minor fall or who have already lost height;

▶ those who have had to take corticosteroids for some time;

▶ heavy smokers or drinkers.

Prevention and treatment

Research has shown that there is a lot you can do to keep your bones strong and healthy:

WEIGHT-BEARING EXERCISE such as walking, dancing or keep-fit makes bones stronger and also improves balance and coordination, which makes falling less likely.

CALCIUM IN THE DIET is vital. Cheese, yogurt and milk are the best sources – skimmed milk is even better than full-fat.

GIVING UP SMOKING AND LIMITING ALCOHOL will help: smoking lowers oestrogen levels and alcohol prevents calcium being absorbed.

HORMONE REPLACEMENT THERAPY (HRT) replaces the oestrogen lost after the menopause. It is available in the form of pills, patches and implants. HRT provides protection against bone loss during the period while you are actually having it. As bone loss occurs at the highest rate immediately after the menopause, having HRT for five or ten years at this time can reduce the risk of fractures in later life by as much as 60 per cent. It also significantly reduces the risk of heart disease. However, HRT is not suitable for everyone: it is thought that long-term use may increase the risk of breast cancer, but research continues in this area.

These preventive measures may benefit people who already suffer from osteoporosis and help prevent further bone loss. Drugs and calcium tablets may also be prescribed. Specialist osteoporosis centres may offer treatments that are not yet available on general prescription.

Physiotherapy may be useful both for pain relief and to increase mobility and help regain muscle strength after a fracture.

 For more information about the causes, prevention and treatment of osteoporosis, including HRT, and a list of specialist osteoporosis centres, contact the National Osteoporosis Society, PO Box 10, Radstock, Bath BA3 3YB. Helpline: 01761 471771.

Phone the Health Helpline on Freephone 0800 66 55 44, weekdays 10am–5pm, for information on common diseases and conditions, NHS services, hospital waiting times, how to make a complaint and how to maintain good health.

See Age Concern Books' *Your Health in Retirement* (details on p 202) for information about other medical conditions, and about the different sorts of practitioner to go to for help.

See Age Concern Books' *Know Your Medicines* (details on p 203) if you or someone you care for wants to know more about medicines you are taking.

Medical insurance

There are two main types of medical insurance scheme:

▶ Comprehensive health plans offer cover for accommodation and treatment in hospital and some care outside the hospital. Schemes offer different levels of protection.

▶ More limited plans may, for example, cover hospital treatment only if it is not available on the NHS within a specified time.

Whatever the policy, the older you are the dearer medical insurance is likely to be. Always compare the details of schemes and look particularly at the exclusions. Many schemes exclude existing conditions.

Long-term care insurance

In the last few years some companies have been offering a new type of insurance policy to cover the costs of long-term care, either in a residential or nursing home or in your own home.

Policies often define six conditions of being able to live a normal life – or Activities of Daily Living (ADLs) – such as washing, feeding and getting dressed. Typically, if you cannot carry out four of these, the policy will pay towards residential or nursing home fees. If you cannot carry out two of them, the policy will pay for help at home. Policies can be designed to pay all the costs of care or to provide a set sum which can be topped up from your resources.

With some schemes you pay regular premiums (which can be very expensive); with others you make a lump-sum payment. People considering such a scheme should seek independent financial advice.

Payments from certain types of long-term care insurance policy are tax-free. Insurance premiums do not qualify for relief.

 Age Concern England has a letter about medical insurance and long-term care insurance which suggests some questions you might want to ask when considering taking out a policy. Send an sae to Age Concern England (address on p 197).

Which? magazine published a report on medical insurance schemes in September 1995 and one on long-term care insurance in February 1997. You should be able to look at these in your local library.

Special needs

The majority of people stay in their own homes and manage to look after themselves until the end of their lives. But some –

▶ **Staying put at home**
▶ **Other housing options**
▶ **Support for carers**

whether because of a disability, a disease or increasing frailty – find they can no longer cope unsupported, particularly if they live alone.

If you have a parent or other older relative who is finding it difficult to cope, you may find yourself in the position of having to make whatever arrangements are necessary to enable them to manage. One option is to make use of the support services that are available to enable them to stay in their own home, if necessary adapting the home to make it more convenient and easy to manage.

Other options are for them to move into housing that offers some support or to move in with you or other relatives. If more day-to-day care is needed than can be provided in any of these settings, then a residential or nursing home might be considered.

Staying put at home

If a person really wants to remain in their own home, but they are not sure if they can go on managing, there may be support services available that would make it possible for them to stay put. There are also various things that can be done to make the home feel safer and more secure, and to make everyday life easier and more comfortable.

Adapting the home

People who suffer from particular disabilities or medical conditions may have difficulty with moving around – getting to the toilet for example – or with routine domestic tasks such as making a cup of tea. There are a lot of simple, straightforward things that can be done to make life easier.

MOBILITY AIDS A walking stick, walking frame, rollator (wheeled frame) or wheelchair might make it easier to move around. All these mobility aids can be obtained free. The hospital physiotherapy or occupational therapy department or the local social services department can give advice.

LAYOUT OF THE HOUSE Are doors easy to open, and wide enough for someone using a wheelchair or walking frame? Are parts of the house so cluttered it is difficult to move around? If the stairs are a problem, grab rails or banisters could be fitted on both sides. Obvious hazards, such as trailing flexes, loose floor coverings or slippery floors, can be removed.

FURNITURE If a person has difficulty getting up from a low chair or bed, a more suitable one could be bought – if you write to the Disabled Living Foundation, they can give advice on this. Repositioning furniture can also help – for example, putting a chair or stool in the bathroom to sit on while drying and dressing.

BATHROOM AND TOILET Securely fixed grab rails and poles can make it much easier to get in and out of the bath or on and off the toilet. Slip-resistant flooring, and a slip-resistant mat in the shower or bath, will reduce the risk of falling. Doors should always open outwards so that if someone falls behind the door it will be easy to reach them.

KITCHEN If this is separate from the dining room, a trolley or a hatch between the rooms might be helpful. Being able to sit down to do certain tasks makes preparing meals less tiring. Units should be easily accessible and within reach. For someone with arthritic hands, there are a number of gadgets available, for example to help with opening tins and jars.

 The Disabled Living Foundation, 380–384 Harrow Road, London W9 2HU, will give advice about special furniture and equipment; just write and ask them what you want to know or ask for details of their free information sheets.

For a list of Disabled Living Centres, where you can go and see the items of equipment that are available, contact the Disabled Living Centres Council, 1st Floor, Winchester House, 11 Cranmer Road, London SW9 6EJ. Tel: 0171-820 0567.

Some branches of Boots now stock personal independence aids, and all branches should have a catalogue. Several disability organisations sell products by mail order.

Keep Able is a large mail order firm that stocks equipment and aids for disabled people. Dial 01784 44 00 44 for a catalogue.

Carers National Association Factsheet 14 *Equipment to aid daily living* is available free from the Carers National Association, 20–25 Glasshouse Yard, London EC1A 4JS (enclose an sae). CarersLine: 0171-490 8898.

RICA (Research Institute for Consumer Affairs) publishes free leaflets on *Equipment for an Easier Life* and *Adapting Your Home*. Both of these include useful address lists. Contact RICA, 2 Marylebone Road, London NW1 4DF. Tel: 0171-935 2460. Textphone: 0171-830 7508.

Help and advice

The best people to give advice are occupational therapists (OTs). OTs assess people's ability to move around and carry out their daily tasks and suggest aids and adaptations to overcome any difficulties. If you have a parent or other older relative who is having difficulties in their day-to-day life because of a disability or medical condition, you could contact the local social services department and ask for the help of an OT.

The OT will also be able to tell you where the nearest Disabled Living Centre is – these are permanent exhibitions where people can try out equipment and receive advice. You can also write to the Disabled Living Foundation for advice. It has its own equipment centre in London, which is open to visitors (appointments needed – phone 0171-289 6111).

Making major alterations

Wider internal doors and a level or ramped approach to the front door will be necessary for anyone who uses a wheelchair, while features such as waist-high electric sockets and a downstairs toilet can make a lot of difference to anyone who has difficulty in moving around.

For anyone who is considering making alterations to their house because they are disabled, an OT will be able to advise on what alterations will be most helpful. Contact the local social services department and ask for the help of an OT. If there is a Care and Repair or Staying Put scheme in the area, they will be able to help you decide what work needs doing and find a suitable architect or builder.

 The Centre for Accessible Environments, Nutmeg House, 60 Gainsford Street, London SE1 2NY. Tel: 0171-357 8182, runs an architectural advisory service, which includes a register of architects and other professionals with experience of designing for older and disabled people.

Financial help with alterations

In addition to the sources of help described on pages 125–126, a **disabled facilities grant** may be available from the local council, depending on income and savings. Disabled facilities grants cover a wider range of work than renovation grants. They will usually be mandatory (which means that the council must give them) if the home needs adaptations to enable someone to get in and out of it or to use essential facilities such as the bathroom, toilet or kitchen.

Feeling secure at home

Telephones

For people who are not able to get out very much or at all, a telephone helps keep in touch with friends and get help in an emergency. Help with the costs of a telephone may be available in certain circumstances, including:

▶ If a person is disabled, the social services department may meet the cost of installation and sometimes the rental. Help with aids and adaptations may also be available.

▶ A person who receives Income Support may be able to get a budgeting loan from the Social Fund (see p 23) to meet installation costs or even to pay a phone bill.

▶ A person who makes very few phone calls may qualify for BT's Light User Scheme. Contact BT on Freephone 150 to enrol.

▶ Deaf and speech-impaired people who have to communicate by text transmission may qualify for the Text Users Rebate Scheme run by the Royal National Institute for Deaf People (RNID).

You could also consider switching to an alternative telephone company that offers cheaper rates.

 If you want information about tinnitus (ringing in the ears) or other hearing problems, contact the Royal National Institute for Deaf People, 19–23 Featherstone Street, London EC1Y 8SL. Tel: 0171-296 8000.

 For further information about help with telephones, see Age Concern Factsheet 28 *Help with telephones*. This includes a list of charities that have in the past provided help with telephone costs to certain categories of people.

DIEL (Advisory Committee on Telecommunications for Disabled and Elderly People) produces an information pack on telephone services for older or disabled people. Contact DIEL, 2nd Floor, Export House, 50 Ludgate Hill, London EC4M 7JJ. Tel: 0171-634 8700.

Dial Freephone 150 for a free copy of *The BT Guide for people who are disabled or elderly*, which gives details of services designed for older or disabled people.

Alarms

Older people may worry about having an accident – falling over, for example – and being unable to call for help, and younger members of their family may worry about them. But people do not have to go into sheltered housing to have 24-hour emergency cover.

It is possible to get an alarm system linked to the telephone. Press a button – either on the phone or on a pendant, clip or wrist strap that is worn all the time – and the call goes straight through to a control centre. Most alarms are two-way: they allow staff at the control centre to speak to you even if you are not near the phone.

If you want to arrange for an older relative to have an alarm installed, you should contact the local housing department and social services department to see if either runs a community alarm scheme, and how much it costs. If they do not have a scheme, you may be able to consider buying an alarm. Those that are not connected to a control centre and do not allow two-way speech are not recommended.

 Ring Age Concern England on 0181-679 8000 for details of its Aid-Call emergency response service.

For more information about alarms, contact the Community Alarms Department at Help the Aged, St James's Walk, London EC1R 0BE. Tel: 0171-253 0253.

 RICA has a booklet called *A Guide to Community Alarms* (£1.95) and the Disabled Living Foundation has a list of alarm systems (addresses on p 171).

Security precautions

There are certain basic steps people can take to make their homes more secure:

► Make sure the outside of the house is well lit.

► Fit good locks on the front and back doors and all accessible windows. Don't ever leave them unlocked when you leave the house.

► Have a door chain and door viewer fitted to the front door, for use when answering the door. Always check the identity of a caller and the purpose of the visit before admitting them to your home. Don't leave the chain in position all the time, as this makes it more difficult to get help in an emergency.

► Don't leave keys to doors or window locks anywhere a burglar might see them.

It is generally not worth the expense of fitting a burglar alarm unless the local Crime Prevention Officer (CPO) advises this. Every police station has a CPO, who will visit people at home and advise them how to make their home more secure.

Some local councils and welfare organisations produce leaflets on security and crime prevention, and a few have special grant schemes to finance security measures. The local Age Concern group, housing department or social services department should know if anything exists in the area. Home repairs assistance might also be available from the local council, as explained on page 125.

FACTFILE

► The older the head of household, the less likely the house is to be burgled.

► In 1993 the likelihood of burglary was 91 per 1,000 households where the head was aged 16–29 and 35 per 1,000 where the head was aged 65 or over.

For more information about security measures see ACE Books' *Your Home in Retirement* (details on p 203) and Age Concern Factsheet 33 *Feeling safer at home and outside.*

Support services

Whether someone needs a couple of hours' help a week – perhaps with shopping – or daily nursing care, being able to get the help they need at home can make all the difference.

Provision of services varies considerably. If you are trying to arrange support services for a parent or other older relative, the local social services department or Age Concern group should know what is available in the area, including schemes that offer help with gardening, decorating, minor repairs and other household tasks, and support groups, for example for people who have had strokes. There may be charges for some or all of these services, depending on income.

Since April 1993 local authorities have had a duty to carry out an assessment of people who appear to them to need community care services which they may arrange. If your relative feels he or she needs such help, you can ask the local authority for an assessment. A decision will then be made on the basis of the assessment about what services – if any – the local authority feels it can offer.

Under the Carers Act 1995, if you are a carer your needs should also be included in the assessment.

Since April 1997 local authorities can give some people (initially they must be under 65) money instead of services, but this money must be used to buy the care they have been assessed as needing. Contact Age Concern England on 0181-679 8000 for more details.

 For more information about support services at home, including the assessment process, see Age Concern Factsheet 6 *Finding help at home.* It includes the addresses of many organisations that might offer help. See also Age Concern Factsheet 32 *Disability and ageing: your right to social services.*

A GP or local Community Health Council should be able to provide information about community health services, arranged either by the Health Authority or by fundholding GPs.

The following is a checklist of some of the services that may be available for older people and people with disabilities:

CHIROPODY Arranged by the Health Authority or fundholding GP (people should ask their own doctor). Also provided by private chiropodists. In some areas nail-cutting is available through the NHS, but this varies.

CONTINENCE ADVICE From trained continence advisers (specialist nurses who advise on problems of incontinence). People should ask their own doctor, or contact the Continence Helpline on 0191-213 0050 – they will be able to give you the name of the local continence adviser.

DAY CARE Care outside a person's home, provided by social services or independent organisations. Some day centres offer specialist care, for example for people with dementia; others offer mainly a chance to meet other people and share activities and a meal.

DISTRICT NURSES Arranged by the Health Authority or fundholding GP (ask your doctor).

HEALTH VISITORS Arranged by the Health Authority or fundholding GP (ask your doctor).

HOME HELP OR HOME CARE Provided by social services, local Age Concern groups, Crossroads and others. Such services may now offer more 'care' rather than the help with household tasks that was traditionally provided.

> Contact the Association of Crossroads Care Attendants Schemes Ltd, 10 Regent Place, Rugby, Warwickshire CV21 2PN. Tel: 01788 573653, to find out if they have a local scheme.

HOSPITAL AFTER-CARE SCHEMES Run by social services and voluntary organisations such as Age Concern.

LAUNDRY SERVICES Run by some social services departments for people with incontinence problems.

LUNCH CLUBS Run by social services or voluntary organisations.

MEALS ON WHEELS Provided by the local council, Age Concern, the Women's Royal Voluntary Service (WRVS) and others.

MOBILE LIBRARIES For people who are housebound.

NIGHT NURSING Provided by the NHS (Health Authority or fundholding GP) or voluntary and private agencies.

OCCUPATIONAL THERAPY Provided by social services, the NHS and private occupational therapists (OTs). OTs assess people's ability to move around and carry out their household tasks and suggest aids and adaptations to overcome any difficulties.

PHYSIOTHERAPY Arranged by the Health Authority or fundholding GP (ask your doctor).

RESPITE CARE Offers carer and person cared for a break from each other, for a day, a night, a week or two weeks. 'Sitting' schemes also enable carers to take a break, either regularly or in emergencies. For information contact the social services department, local Age Concern group, local carers' group, your GP, or the local Alzheimer's Disease Society group.

TRANSPORT SCHEMES (EG DIAL-A-RIDE) Arranged by social services and voluntary organisations (see pp 93–94).

VISITING SCHEMES Run by social services and voluntary organisations.

Other housing options

AT A GLANCE

- Moving to special housing
- Living with relatives or friends
- Moving to a residential or nursing home

People who find it difficult to manage on their own, despite whatever help is available to them in their own homes, may prefer to move to some sort of special housing. Another option for some older people is to move in with a younger relative or friend. If neither of these options provides sufficient day-to-day care, a move to a residential or nursing home may be the answer.

Moving to special housing

People may move into special housing for many reasons: they may not be able to get all the support they need at home; their own home may really not be suitable for their needs; they may like the idea of having someone on call if they need help.

There are various types of special housing available to suit different needs. These include:

▶ housing specially designed for older people, but without a warden (see pp 113–114);

▶ retirement housing, with a warden, often called a scheme manager (see pp 114–115);

▶ an almshouse (see pp 119–120);

▶ an Abbeyfield Society house;

▶ extra-care retirement housing;

▶ housing for disabled people.

Abbeyfield houses

Local Abbeyfield Societies all over the country manage over 1,000 houses between them, mostly with 7 to 12 residents. Residents have their own bedsitting rooms with their own furniture; they come together for the main meals of the day, which are prepared by a resident house-keeper. Abbeyfield houses are popular for the combination of privacy and family-type atmosphere which they provide. The Abbeyfield Society also has some 'extra-care' houses where a greater degree of care and support is available.

Abbeyfield residents are usually considered to be licensees rather than tenants in the same way as the residents of almshouses (see pp 119–120).

 Details of your nearest Abbeyfield house can be obtained from the Abbeyfield Society, 53 Victoria Street, St Albans, Hertfordshire AL1 3UW. Tel: 01727 857536.

Extra-care retirement housing

Some councils and housing associations offer retirement housing with additional services such as the provision of meals and care assistants. Nursing care is generally not provided. This type of housing is also known as 'very sheltered housing' or 'housing with care'. Unfortunately there is not much of it available, and almost none to buy. Contact your local council and housing associations for information.

Extra care can also be provided within ordinary retirement housing schemes, as explained on page 115.

 For more about the different types of retirement housing, see Age Concern Books' *A Buyer's Guide to Retirement Housing* (details on p 203).

Housing for disabled people

Many councils and housing associations now have a few properties that are specially built for people who use a wheelchair or have problems getting around. This may be referred to as **mobility housing** or **wheelchair housing**. A few councils and housing associations build **lifetime homes,** which are designed to be adaptable to people's changing needs.

Living with relatives or friends

If you are thinking of having an older relative or friend to live with you, you should always weigh the pros and cons carefully. It is all too easy to enter into such arrangements without either party realising how much their independence may be affected. These are some of the points that are worth considering:

▶ Is your home conveniently situated for shops, transport and so on? It will probably not suit you or your relative if you find yourself having to drive them everywhere they want to go.

▶ Where will their room be? Unless they have a downstairs room, there is always a risk that they may come to find the stairs difficult and end up staying longer in their room than they want to, or staying downstairs longer than they want to once they have got down.

▶ Is there a decent-sized spare room, so that you and they will be able to invite friends to stay?

▶ If you have children at home, will your relative find actually living with them too much, however fond of the children they are?

▶ What are the arrangements for washing, cleaning and so on?

▶ What happens if your relative starts to need more day-to-day care? They may be totally independent at first, but this could change. If you have discussed these possibilities before they move in, at least you will all have gone into the arrangement with your eyes open.

A granny flat or annexe

Having a parent or other older relative living in a self-contained 'granny' flat or annexe linked to your home can be an ideal arrangement, but problems can arise. The crucial thing is that you should both have similar expectations about how much time you are going to spend together, how much time they are going to spend looking after their grandchildren, and so on. If expectations do not match, it is likely that one party will end up feeling guilty and the other resentful.

Welfare benefits

If a person is receiving social security benefits such as Income Support or Attendance Allowance, they are likely to go on receiving them if they move in with you. However, they will not be able to receive Housing Benefit towards any rent they pay you unless they live separately, either in a 'granny flat' or in the same house but only sharing areas such as hall and bathroom.

 For information about benefits for people with low incomes and benefits for disabled people, see pages 20–27.

Legal arrangements

However good an arrangement seems, circumstances can change, or you may simply not get on as well as you had hoped.

If an older relative puts money into buying a property with you, or into improvements or adaptations to your existing home, they should have a legal share in the property – though this could pose serious problems for you if they ever have to go into a residential or nursing home.

 See Age Concern Factsheet 38 *Treatment of the former home as capital for people in residential and nursing homes* for information about how the value of your property is treated if other people are still living there.

On the other hand, you may want to have an agreement which enables you to ask them to leave if certain conditions are breached. You might also want to retain sole ownership of your home.

Moving to a residential or nursing home

The difference between residential and nursing homes lies in the type of care that is provided.

RESIDENTIAL HOMES provide day-to-day personal care but not nursing care. They are run by local authorities, or by voluntary and private organisations, which have to be registered with the local authority. The local social services department will have a list of homes in the area.

NURSING HOMES provide 24-hour nursing care. Almost all are privately run. They must be registered with the Health Authority, which will have a list of homes in the area.

DUAL-REGISTERED HOMES are registered for residential and nursing care. In such homes, people will not have to move if they come to need more or less care.

When choosing a home, it is advisable to look at more than one if possible. Here are some questions it might be worth asking:

► How much choice does the home offer residents about aspects of everyday life such as what and when they eat, when and where they see visitors, when they get up and go to bed?

► Do residents have the choice of single or shared rooms? If rooms are shared, can they choose who they share with?

► Can residents bring any personal possessions with them – pictures, plants, furniture?

► Do residents have the use of a telephone in privacy?

► Is there more than one living room, a quiet one as well as one with a television? Are there smoking and non-smoking rooms?

► Can wheelchairs go everywhere in the home? Is there a lift?

► Does the home arrange to take residents out to the shops, to the theatre and other entertainments, to places of worship?

► Is there a residents' committee?

► Does the home encourage residents to make comments or complaints about the home?

It is always a good idea for a prospective resident to have a trial stay before making a final decision.

 Age Concern Factsheet 29 *Finding residential and nursing home accommodation* includes a list of organisations that provide information and advice. See also Age Concern Books' *Caring in a Crisis: Finding and paying for residential and nursing home care* (details on p 201).

Paying for care in homes

For people wishing to enter a care home or anyone who has entered a home since 1 April 1993 there are basically three options:

1 People who can afford to can find and pay for a home for themselves. They can claim Attendance Allowance or Disability Living Allowance (DLA). If their money subsequently runs low, they can apply to the local authority, as under option 2. If financially supported by the local authority on a permanent basis, they will stop receiving Attendance Allowance or the care component of DLA after four weeks.

2 People who need residential care but cannot afford it have to approach the local authority for assessment of their needs to see whether the local authority will agree to place them in a home. If the local authority agrees, it pays the cost of the place and then collects as much as possible of that cost from the resident. Residents with savings and capital of more than £16,000 have to pay the fees themselves (but in certain circumstances the value of their home may be ignored). Those with £16,000 or less have their income and savings assessed to see how much they have to pay themselves. They will be encouraged to make up their income by claiming all the benefits they are entitled to, including Income Support and residential allowance, which is paid as part of Income Support to people who qualify on financial grounds. (People entering a local authority home generally cannot claim Income Support.) If someone wishes to live in a more expensive home than the local authority is willing to pay for, they must pay the extra fees through a third party.

3 People who need continuing nursing care which they cannot afford may have their care arranged by the local authority or the Health Authority. If care is arranged by the Health Authority, no means test is required. If the local authority arranges the care, the assessment process is the same as under option 2. The Health Authority must approve nursing home placements made by the local authority.

When one of a couple enters a care home, then the local authority will assess how much the resident must pay towards the fees solely on the resident's savings and income. However, the spouse is regarded as a 'liable relative' and may be asked to contribute towards the cost.

If a resident has an occupational or personal pension and a spouse living at home, the local authority will ignore half the pension when assessing the resident's income provided that they pass at least this amount to their spouse.

 For further information, see Age Concern Factsheet 10 *Local authority charging procedures for residential and nursing home care* and Factsheet 39 *Paying for care in a residential or nursing home if you have a partner.*

People who were already permanently resident in a private or voluntary home on 31 March 1993 are covered by what is known as 'preserved rights' to special rates of Income Support – the old system. People permanently resident in a local authority home before that date, or sponsored by the local authority in other homes, have been reassessed under the new procedure described above.

 For further information see Age Concern Factsheet 11 *Financial support for people in residential and nursing homes prior to 1 April 1993.*

For information about television licence concessions for disabled people and people over pension age living in residential or nursing homes or some types of retirement housing, see Age Concern Factsheet 3 *Television licence concessions.*

Support for carers

Caring for someone over a long period of time can affect the health of the carer. Irritability, headaches, constant tiredness, loss of appetite, depression and tearfulness can all be symptoms of stress. If you care for a relative or friend and are beginning to suffer from stress of this sort, you should seek help, both for your sake and for the sake of the person you care for. You could contact the Carers National Association, which has local groups all over the country. Your local Age Concern group or social services department should also be able to tell you whether there is a carers' support group in the area. Sharing your problems will probably be a relief in itself.

Since April 1996, carers have the right to ask for their own needs to be assessed when the person for whom they care is being assessed. Those doing the assessment should not assume that you are willing to go on caring, or to continue providing the same level of care as you have been doing.

Contact the Carers National Association, 20–25 Glasshouse Yard, London EC1A 4JS. CarersLine: 0171-490 8898, for the address of your nearest group, or for advice and support.

In addition, a GP or social worker may be able to organise practical support:

▶ A home help, home care worker or sitting service may be organised to enable you to get out or have some time to yourself.

▶ The person you look after may be able to have some day care.

▶ Respite care may be arranged for a few days or even a week or two to give you a break.

Chapter 1 describes various sorts of financial help available to people who look after a severely disabled person for 35 hours a week or more. Invalid Care Allowance is described on page 27. If you receive Income Support you may qualify for the carer's premium, as explained on page 21. Finally, if you receive Invalid Care Allowance, or you qualify for it but do not receive it because you are already receiving another benefit, you will receive National Insurance credits to protect your State Pension.

See page 110 for information about holidays for carers.

Age Concern Books' *Caring in a Crisis: What to do and who to turn to* and the other books in the *Caring in a Crisis* series are specially written for anyone who is involved in caring for a relative or friend (details on pp 201–202).

Bereavement

- ▶ **Coping with grief**
- ▶ **Practical arrangements to be made after a death**

The death of someone we love deeply is probably the most devastating experience that will ever happen to us. People have described it as feeling like 'being cut in half'. In addition to these overwhelming emotions, our lives may seem to be thrown into turmoil, with both our day-to-day routine and our hopes and plans for the future completely overturned. This section looks at both the process of grieving itself and the practical arrangements that need to be made immediately after a death.

Coping with grief

Mourning is essential to our well-being and our recovery. We need to allow ourselves time to mourn: blocking our feelings only delays the process of healing. Eventually we will reach a time when existence acquires some meaning again and it becomes possible to start to rebuild our lives.

The stages of grief

Though each person's reaction to bereavement is unique, grief does usually have an overall pattern. Most of us will go through the stages of shock and disbelief, intense sadness and pain, regrets, longings, depression, perhaps anger, aggression and guilt. We do not all experience all these feelings, nor do we experience them in the same order or with the same intensity. It may nevertheless be reassuring to know that all these feelings are shared by many others, and that they will not last for ever.

SHOCK AND DISBELIEF are usually the first reactions. You may feel numb and unreal, especially if the death has been sudden and unexpected. The reality of the funeral can help you begin to accept that the person you love has died.

THE FEELING OF LOSS can at times be so overwhelming that you may almost feel you are breaking down or going mad. Symptoms such as loss of appetite, sleeplessness, exhaustion, restlessness and feelings of panic are all common. It is important to try to eat sensibly and generally look after yourself, however little you may feel like it.

ANGER AND AGGRESSION can also be expressions of grief. Death can seem cruel and unfair, especially if the person has died young. You may rail against God or fate, against those responsible for the death, against yourself for being unable to prevent it, against the person who has died for leaving you in the lurch. You may feel resentful towards other people who have not experienced a loss: 'Why did this happen to me and not them?'

FEELINGS OF GUILT are also common, and can be very destructive. You may hold yourself partly to blame for the death: 'If only I had called the doctor sooner.' Things left undone and unsaid may loom very large in your mind.

DEPRESSION, DESPAIR AND APATHY will probably at some stage beset anyone who has lost someone they love. Life without them may seem pointless, and getting through each day may be a struggle. But if the depression never seems to lift, you should see your doctor: you might be suffering from clinical depression, which can be treated.

REMEMBERING AND RELIVING THE PAST is part of grieving. Although this may at first be painful, it can bring back happy memories, which can be very comforting.

Some people find it easier to show their feelings than others, but most find at some stage that it helps to talk – whether to family, friends, your local priest or a trained bereavement counsellor.

Signs of recovery

When you first suffer a bereavement, it seems almost impossible to imagine that the pain will ever get any less, that you will ever again be without a lump in your throat and a knot in your stomach. Then after a time – and no one can dictate how long that time should be – you realise that a few hours have passed and you haven't thought of the person you have lost. You may at first feel guilty about this: it seems almost a betrayal that you can forget in this way. But it is wrong to feel guilty: this is the beginning of recovery. You are gradually accepting the reality that the person you loved is gone, that they are part of your past and you still have a life ahead of you to be lived.

There will of course be ups and downs, and periods when things seem to be getting worse not better. At first you may well find family occasions and festivals such as Christmas and New Year particularly sad. Setbacks like this are inevitable, but slowly and surely the process of healing will go on.

If the person who has died is your partner of many years, one long-term effect is often loneliness. You may miss their physical presence, the intimacy, having someone always on hand to talk to and do things with. Living alone may seem almost unbearable, and the effort required to build up a new life impossibly great.

Talking to people who have themselves lost a partner may help. Cruse – Bereavement Care has volunteer counsellors all over the country who can talk on the telephone, answer letters or visit people at home. Local branches also organise regular social meetings for bereaved people.

For more information about what Cruse offers, contact them at Cruse House, 126 Sheen Road, Richmond, Surrey TW9 1UR. Tel: 0181-940 4818. Cruse also has a Bereavement Line on 0181-332 7227, weekdays 9.30am–5pm.

Practical arrangements to be made after a death

When someone we love dies we may feel we just want to crawl away and hide like a wounded animal, but we usually have to face all sorts of practical problems. The most immediate tasks are registering the death and arranging the funeral. In addition the dead person's Will (if there is one) may have to be 'proved', and their property disposed of in accordance with it.

Registering the death

A death should be registered within five days, normally by a close relative. The doctor or hospital will usually give the nearest relative or person present at the death a certificate giving the cause of death. If the body is to be cremated, two doctors must sign the certificate. You should take this to the Registrar of Births and Deaths for the district where the death occurred, together with the medical card and any war pension book of the person who has died, if available.

In addition to the date and place of death, the registrar will need to know the full names of the person who has died, their date and place of birth, and their most recent occupation (and that of her husband in the case of a married woman). Once the register is signed, the registrar will issue you with:

▶ a certificate of disposal (green), to be given to the funeral director;

▶ a certificate of registration (white), used for claiming social security benefits;

▶ the death certificate (£2.50 in 1997), which will be needed for dealing with the estate of the person who has died.

If a death occurs suddenly or unexpectedly the coroner must be informed. He or she will decide whether it is necessary to hold a post mortem.

 For more information see DSS leaflet D 49 *What to Do After a Death.*

Arranging the funeral

If you are arranging a funeral, always check whether the dead person left any instructions about the funeral, or had taken out any kind of funeral prepayment plan (see p 56). If you do not have the means to pay for even a simple funeral, and there is insufficient money in the dead person's estate, you may qualify for a Funeral Payment from the Social Fund, as explained on page 23.

Always get a written, itemised estimate of all the costs involved – funeral directors accept that relatives are likely to get several quotations before deciding which company to use.

The funeral director can arrange for the body to be taken to a chapel of rest once the death has been certified. He or she must have the burial or cremation certificates before the funeral can take place.

Everyone has the right to a church funeral, and to burial in the churchyard of the parish in which they die – provided there is one and there is space in it. An alternative is to be buried in a cemetery, usually run by the local authority. It is not necessary to have a service for a burial or a cremation: a relative or friend can say a few words, or a non-religious ceremony can be held.

 For more information about all aspects of arranging a funeral, see Age Concern Factsheet 27 *Arranging a funeral.* As Scottish law is different from English law, Scottish readers should contact Age Concern Scotland (address on p 197) for further information.

 For advice and help with a non-religious ceremony, contact the British Humanist Association (Tel: 0171-430 0908) or the National Secular Society (Tel: 0171-404 3126), both at 47 Theobald's Road, London WC1X 8SP.

Dealing with probate

When a person dies their assets may be frozen until probate is granted. No one, not even a spouse, will then be able to draw money from their bank account (unless it is a joint account). The responsibility for obtaining probate falls to the 'personal representative' of the person who has died.

The personal representative

The 'personal representative' of the person who has died is responsible for dealing with their money, property and possessions. The personal representative is usually the person named in the Will as executor. If there is no executor or the executor cannot or will not act, someone is appointed as administrator of the estate – either the main beneficiary of the Will or a close relative. If the estate is complicated or the Will is likely to be contested, the personal representative should consider using a solicitor.

The personal representative can deduct his or her expenses from the estate, but only a professional executor can be paid for the work involved in dealing with the estate.

The grant of representation

The personal representative needs a formal legal document from the High Court to prove that he or she has the authority to deal with the assets of the dead person. In effect a grant of representation transfers all the money and property of the person who has died to the personal representative, to distribute according to the instructions set out in the Will or according to the intestacy rules (explained on p 56). The document is called a grant of probate when issued to an executor who has 'proved' the Will. An administrator is given a grant of letters of administration.

A grant of representation may not be needed if:

▶ The estate is made up entirely of cash and personal possessions.

▶ All the property in the estate is owned in joint names as joint tenants: this means the property automatically becomes wholly owned by the surviving joint tenant.

- All assets are held in joint names.
- The total amount of savings is less than £5,000.
- A 'nomination agreement' exists (these could only be made before 1981).

If you do need to apply for a grant, the local Probate Registry will provide you with application forms and a leaflet (PA 2) entitled *How to Obtain Probate*. As personal representative you will have to complete several forms, including:

THE PROBATE APPLICATION (FORM PA 1) This gives details about the person who has died, the surviving relatives, the personal representative and the Will.

A RETURN OF THE WHOLE ESTATE (FORM CAP 44) This asks for details of the estate and its value and is used to prepare the account for the Inland Revenue, as Inheritance Tax may have to be paid.

In order to complete the necessary forms you will have to obtain information on:

- the value at the date of death of all assets owned by the dead person;
- any money owed to the dead person;
- any debts owed by the dead person, including tax.

The completed forms, together with the death certificate, the original Will and all relevant supporting documents such as letters confirming the value of assets, should be sent to the local Probate Registry.

Once the Probate Registry has prepared all the legal documents, you will be asked to come for an interview, to confirm the details you have given. You will have to pay a fee based on the value of the estate. You may also order extra official copies of the grant of representation to send to institutions holding assets of the dead person – usually an ordinary photocopy is not acceptable.

Paying Inheritance Tax

You have to pay Inheritance Tax (see p 32) before probate/administration is granted, but it is not always possible to use money from the estate to pay it until you have the grant of representation. You may therefore need to raise money to pay both Inheritance Tax and probate fees. You may be able to obtain the funds from money held by the dead person in National Savings investments or Government stocks, or from a bank or building society account, if the institution concerned agrees.

It is advisable to open a separate bank or building society account, known as an 'executorship account', to which all money paid into the estate can be credited. If this is done, the bank or building society will often agree to lend the money to pay the tax and probate fees, provided the estate is of sufficient value to cover the loan.

Settling the estate

Once all the application procedures have been completed, and Inheritance Tax and probate fees paid, the grant of representation will be issued in the form of the probate/administration document.

You can now begin to settle the estate and arrange for the distribution of property and possessions. You will need to do the following:

- ► Obtain all the assets belonging to the estate, sending a copy of the grant to each institution holding assets.
- ► Advertise formally for creditors, if the personal representative is not also the main beneficiary.
- ► Pay the outstanding debts of the estate – if there seems to be insufficient money to pay all the debts you should seek legal advice.
- ► Finalise the payment of taxes.
- ► Dispose of any unwanted property, in particular by selling anything of value.
- ► Distribute the estate either according to the terms of the Will or under the intestacy rules if there is no Will.

When distributing the assets, you should obtain a signed receipt from each beneficiary. Once all specific bequests have been made, you should prepare estate accounts. The residue or remainder of the estate can then be transferred to the main beneficiary.

 For more details see Age Concern Factsheet 14 *Probate: dealing with someone's estate*. As Scottish law is different from English law, Scottish readers should contact Age Concern Scotland (address on p 197).

About Age Concern

The Retirement Handbook is one of a wide range of publications produced by Age Concern England – the National Council on Ageing. In addition, Age Concern is actively engaged in training, information provision, research and campaigning for retired people and those who work with them. It is a registered charity dependent on public support for the continuation of its work.

Age Concern England links closely with Age Concern centres in Scotland, Wales and Northern Ireland to form a network of over 1,400 independent local UK groups. These groups, with the invaluable help of an estimated 250,000 volunteers, aim to improve the quality of life for older people and develop services appropriate to local needs and resources. These include advice and information, day care, visiting services, transport schemes, clubs, and specialist facilities for physically and mentally frail older people.

Age Concern England
Astral House
1268 London Road
London SW16 4ER

Tel: 0181-679 8000

Age Concern Scotland
113 Rose Street
Edinburgh EH2 3DT

Tel: 0131-220 3345

Age Concern Cymru
4th Floor
1 Cathedral Road
Cardiff CF1 9SD

Tel: 01222 371566

Age Concern Northern Ireland
3 Lower Crescent
Belfast BT7 1NR
Tel: 01232 245729

Publications from Age Concern Books

Money matters

Your Rights: A guide to money benefits for older people

Sally West

A highly acclaimed annual guide to the State benefits available to older people. Contains current information on Income Support, Housing Benefit, Retirement Pensions, Incapacity Benefit and Jobseeker's Allowance, among other things, and advice on how to claim them.

For further information please telephone 0181-679 8000

Your Taxes and Savings: A guide for older people

Sally West and the Money Management Council

This definitive annual guide to financial planning provides a comprehensive explanation of the impact of taxation on the finances of older people. It also looks at managing retirement income and evaluates the wide range of investment opportunities available. Advice is given on building an investment portfolio and seven model portfolios are included.

For further information please telephone 0181-679 8000

The Pensions Handbook: A mid-career guide to improving retirement income

Sue Ward

Many older people in their later working lives become concerned about the adequacy of their existing pension arrangements. This title addresses these worries and suggests strategies by which the value of a prospective pension can be enhanced. Advice is also provided on monitoring company pension schemes.

For further information please telephone 0181-679 8000

Using Your Home as Capital
Cecil Hinton

This best-selling book for homeowners, which is updated annually, gives a detailed explanation of how to capitalise on the value of your home and obtain a regular additional income.

For further information please telephone 0181-679 8000

Earning Money in Retirement
Kenneth Lysons

Many people, for a variety of reasons, wish to continue in some form of paid employment beyond the normal retirement age. This helpful guide explores the practical implications of such a choice and highlights some of the opportunities available.

£3.99 0–86242–103–9

FORTHCOMING – TO BE PUBLISHED SPRING 1998

Managing Other People's Money (2nd edition)
Penny Letts

The management of money and property is usually a personal and private matter. However, there may come a time when someone else has to take over on either a temporary or a permanent basis. This book looks at the circumstances in which such a need could arise and provides a step-by-step guide to the arrangements which have to be made.

0–86242–250–7

Managing Debt
Rex Mottershead

Based on personal experience, and written in clear layperson's language, this book guides the reader through the essential aspects of debt, including the legal processes, dealings with creditors, and strategies for getting organised. In addition, the appendices contain a range of model letters which will prove invaluable for dealing with a variety of creditors.

£6.99 0–86242–236–1

General

Changing Direction: Employment options in mid-life
Sue Ward
Redundancy or early retirement can come as a shock to anybody, but the impact in mid-life can be devastating. This topical and highly practical book is designed to help those aged 40–55 get back to work. Always positive and upbeat, it examines issues such as adjusting to change, finances, opportunities for work, deciding what work you really want to do and working for yourself.
£6.95   0–86242–190–X

The World at Your Feet: A traveller's guide for women in mid-life and beyond
Nina Hathway
This comprehensive and detailed guide is packed full of advice and guidance on every aspect of travelling for older women. Designed to be *the* book for women with adventure in their hearts, it is full of valuable information, including how to decide on a suitable trip, being prepared, keeping safe and healthy, meeting other people and enjoying your own company.
£6.95   0–86242–189–6

Separation and Divorce: A guide for women in mid-life and beyond
Tobe Aleksander
Older women face particular problems when experiencing the breakup of their relationship and when considering separation or divorce. This book helps women look at what has happened in their relationships and examine the options open to them. It also provides a practical guide through the legal and financial maze they will encounter, with a step-by-step description of the divorce process and the procedures of the Child Support Agency. The experiences of women who have gone through separation and divorce are included throughout the book.
£7.95   0–86242–173–X

An Active Retirement
Nancy Tuft
Bursting with information on hobbies, sports, educational opportunities and voluntary work, this practical guide is ideal for retired people seek-

ing new ways to fill their time but uncertain where to start.
£5.33 0–86242–119–5

Eating Well on a Budget

Sara Lewis

Completely revised, the new edition of this successful title offers sound advice on shopping and cooking cost-effectively and includes wholesome original recipes for four complete weekly menus.
£4.66 0–86242–120–9

Healthy Eating on a Budget

Sara Lewis and Dr Juliet Gray

This book shows how, even on a tight budget, it is possible to produce meals that are both healthy and delicious. Opening with a comprehensive introduction to achieving a nutritionally balanced diet, there are 100 plus closely costed recipes for the health-conscious cook, all of which are flagged up to show their nutritional values and calorie content.
£6.95 0–86242–170–5

Living, Loving and Ageing: Sexual and personal relationships in later life

Wendy Greengross and Sally Greengross

Sexuality is often regarded as the preserve of the younger generation. This book, for older people and those who work with them, tackles the issues in a straightforward fashion, avoiding preconceptions and bias.
£4.95 0–86242–070–9

Health and care

THE CARING IN A CRISIS SERIES

The 'Caring in a Crisis' series has been written for the families and friends of older people. It guides you through the key stages of a crisis and helps you take practical, informed decisions.

What to do and who to turn to

Marina Lewycka £6.95 0–86242–166–7

Finding and paying for residential and nursing home care

Marina Lewycka £6.95 0–86242–157–8

Going home from hospital
Sheila White £6.95 0–86242–155–1

Caring for someone who is dying
Penny Mares £6.95 0–86242–158–6

Caring for someone who has dementia
Jane Brotchie £6.95 0–86242–182–9

Caring for someone who has had a stroke
Philip Coyne with Penny Mares £6.95 0–86242–183–7

Choices for the carer of an elderly relative
Marina Lewycka £6.95 0–86242–184–5

FORTHCOMING – TO BE PUBLISHED AUTUMN 1997

Caring at a distance
Julie Spencer-Cingoz £6.99 0–86242–228–0

Caring for someone with alcohol problems
Mike Ward £6.99 0–86242–227–2

The Foot Care Book: An A–Z of fitter feet
Judith Kemp SRCh
A self-help guide for elderly people on routine foot care, this book includes an A–Z of problems relating to choosing and adapting shoes and a guide to who's who in foot care.
£1.99 0–86242–066–0

In Control: Help with incontinence
Penny Mares
Containing information about the nature and causes of incontinence and the sources of help available, this book has been written for anyone concerned about such a problem, either professionally or at home. The text is illustrated throughout with diagrams and case histories.
£3.46 0–86242–088–1

Your Health in Retirement
Dr J A Muir Gray and Pat Blair
This book is a comprehensive source of information to help readers look after themselves and work towards better health. Produced in easy-

to-read A–Z style, full details are given of people and useful organisations from which advice and assistance can be sought.
£3.34 0–86242–082–2

Know Your Medicines (3rd edition)
Pat Blair
We would all like to know more about the medicines we take. The third edition of this successful guide is written for older people and their carers and examines how the body works and the effects of medication.
0–86242–226–4

Housing

A Buyer's Guide to Retirement Housing
Co-published with the NHTPC
Buying a flat or bungalow in a sheltered scheme? This new edition of this successful guide provides vital information on the running costs, location, design and management of schemes to help you make an informed decision.
£4.95 0–86242–127–6

An Owner's Guide: Your home in retirement
Co-published with the NHTPC
This definitive guide considers all aspects of home maintenance of concern to retired people and those preparing for retirement, providing advice on heating, insulation and adaptations.
£1.68 0–86242–095–4

Housing Options for Older People
David Bookbinder
A review of housing options is part of growing older. All the possibilities and their practical implications are carefully considered in this comprehensive guide.
£3.32 0–86242–108–X

Age Well publications

Age Well Handbook: Setting up community health initiatives for older people

Caroline Nash and Tony Carter

Gives practical advice on how to introduce health-related activities from peer health counselling to arts projects. It provides guidance for those who feel that ageing and retirement need not mean inactivity, and that health and well-being can and should be enjoyed by people of all ages.
£2.00 0–86242–116–0

Age Well Planning and Ideas Pack

To provide guidelines, ideas and sources of information to those interested in planning and developing health promotion activities with older people.

Available on receipt of a 9″ × 12″ sae:

Single copy   49p stamp
2 copies   93p stamp
3 copies   £1.40 stamp

For larger orders, up to a maximum of 10 copies, please enclose a cheque (made payable to Age Concern England) to cover parcel post, as follows:

4 copies   £2.60
5 to 9 copies £3.25
10 copies   £4.25

To order books, send a cheque or money order for the appropriate amount, payable to Age Concern England, to the address below. Postage and packing are free. Credit card orders may be made on 0181-679 8000.

Mail Order Unit
Age Concern England, 1268 London Road, London SW16 4ER

Information factsheets

Age Concern England produces over 30 factsheets on a variety of subjects, which are revised and updated throughout the year. Single copies are available free on receipt of a 9″ × 12″ sae. For information about charges for multiple copies and about the annual subscription service, or to order factsheets, write to the Information Services Division, Age Concern England, 1268 London Road, London SW16 4ER.

Index